The Breaking of Bread

THE BREAKING OF BREAD

A RECONSTRUCTION OF THE ORDER FOLLOWED BY THE FIRST CHURCH OF JERUSALEM

FIRST CHURCH OF JERUSALEM

Published by First Church of Jerusalem

First edition 2020

Cover illustration: "The Last Supper"
by Pascal Dagnan-Bouveret, 1896
(detail)

All Bible texts quoted are from the
New King James Version unless otherwise stated.

ISBN 978-0-9933599-2-7

www.firstchurchofjerusalem.global

ON THIS ROCK I WILL BUILD MY CHURCH, AND THE GATES OF HADES SHALL NOT PREVAIL AGAINST IT.

JESUS CHRIST

CONTENTS

INTRODUCTION

"Do this in remembrance of Me."

Luke 22:19

This service is a speculative reconstruction of the celebration inaugurated by Christ at the Last Supper, as practiced by the first believers, and known initially as the Breaking of Bread (e.g. Acts 2:46). As the progenitor of the Eucharistic services we are familiar with today, including the Divine Liturgy, the Mass, and the Holy Communion, this early celebration of thanksgiving (Gk. 'eucharistia') is the common heritage of all believers, and will be of interest to those who seek a greater understanding and experience of the historic roots of their faith. It is here presented in a form suitable for contemporary use.

The significance of the Breaking of Bread for the first believers can only be fully understood in the context of their relationship with Christ. Many of them had seen, heard or met Jesus personally during His earthly life, many had seen Him and heard Him teach after His resurrection and prior to His ascension into heaven, and all had received the Holy Spirit through whom Christ continued to be present with them. Jesus had Himself taught the centrality of relationship with God, making it clear that this was a personal and experiential reality available for all believers to experience and enjoy.

In fulfilment of Divine prophecy Jesus was born into the people chosen by God, a people called to that place of inner silence, faith, and rest, in which His love may be known and His voice heard. Although Israel had failed to live out these values as a nation, they were nevertheless enshrined forever at its heart. Their scriptures were themed by loving and seeking God (e.g., Genesis 5:22-24; 6:9; Exodus 5:22-6:3; Leviticus 19:1-4; Numbers 11:29; Deuteronomy

4:29; 6:5; 1 Chronicles 16:10,11; 22:19; 28:9; 2 Chronicles 7:14; 11:16; 12:14; 14:14; 15:2,12,13; 19:3; 20:3,4; 30:19; 31:21; 34:3; Ezra 6:21; 8:21,22; Job 5:8; Psalm 9:10; 10:4; 14:2; 22:26; 24:6; 27:4,8; 34:10; 40:16; 46:10; 53:2; 63:1; 69:6,32; 70:4; 83:16; 105:3,4; 119:2; Proverbs 1:28; 8:17; 28:5; Isaiah 8:19; 9:13; 26:9: 31:1; 51:1; 55:6; 58:2; Jeremiah 29:13; 50:4; Lamentations 3:25; Daniel 9:3; Hosea 3:5; 5:6,15; 7:10; 10:12; Amos 5:4,6,8; Habakkuk 2:1-3; Zephaniah 2:3; Zechariah 8:21,22; Malachi 3:1). Christ proclaimed the glorious message that God may be known. From the beginning of His earthly ministry, this was His cry: 'Repent, for the kingdom of heaven is at hand!' (Matthew 4:17).

Encouraging His hearers to seek God (Matthew 6:33; Luke 11:9-13; 12:31), Jesus sought to draw them into that loving relationship offered by the Father from of old (Matthew 22:37,38; Mark 12:30; John 15:9). His purpose was that they might know Him (Isaiah 43:10), be united with Him (John 17:20-23), and abundantly experience His life (John 10:10), all of which would be amply provided through the central event of all human history, the sacrifice of the Cross (John 3:14; 12:32; Hebrews 9:11-28).

Christ called all to an experiential relationship with the Trinity. At His meeting with the Pharisee Nicodemus He explains how this can be, assuring him that such a relationship is impossible unless one is born again of the Spirit of God (John 3:3-8). As a teacher of Israel Nicodemus should have known this (John 3:10). Salvation was as available to those who looked forward to the Cross as to those who would look back to it (Job 19:25). Through faith in the Messiah, the Son of Man, the spirit of the believer is regenerated by God, and being spiritually reborn in this way, he or she from that moment 'sees' the kingdom of God (John 3:3). The Greek term here translated 'see' describes not merely the physical sense of sight but 'to personally know, i.e. to have seen or have experienced something by first hand observation' (Mickelson/Strong, 2015). There can be no ambiguity, no doubt, no question. Jesus is talking about experience, making it clear that it is normative for everyone who places their faith in Him to experience God as present with them, walking and talking with them each day.

'Abide in Me,' He says (John 15:4-11). This is nothing less than a Divine call to communion and communication. 'Abide in My word,' He says (John 8:31), which cannot be an admonition to read the gospels, for they had not yet been written! Rather, it is an admonition to hear His word, take it to heart and follow it. During His earthly life, only those within earshot could hear the Lord Jesus Christ, but after the outpouring of the Holy Spirit at Pentecost, He was present with every believer, fulfilling His promise that He would be with us always (Matthew 28:20). We who never heard Him when He walked on earth as a man may now daily look to Him (Hebrews 12:2), hear Him speak personally to us, and talk with Him as one talks with their friend. This is He who says, 'My sheep hear My voice, and I know them, and they follow Me' (John 10:27).

Jesus was emphatic in emphasising the primacy and pre-eminence of seeking God, just as His spiritual forebears had done before Him. When Mary sat in silence at His feet whilst her sister Martha served, He took the opportunity to teach this timeless principle, insisting that in choosing to sit at His feet and listen to Him, Mary had done the one thing that was needed. She chose that good part, which would never be taken away from her (Luke 10:38-42).

This was the culture of the first church. It was a hesychastic society with Christ at its centre, the proper object of contemplation, devotion, and dependence. Through their faith in Christ as Saviour they entered the rest from which all good flows (Hebrews 4:2,3), and from that rest issued the mighty works of God (Acts 2:43), works finished from the foundation of the world (Hebrews 4:3). He Himself had said to them, 'Come to Me, all you who labour and are heavy laden, and I will give you rest. Take My yoke upon you and learn from Me, for I am gentle and lowly in heart, and you will find rest for your souls. For My yoke is easy and

My burden is light' (Matthew 11:28-30). Resting from their own labours, they entered into God's, for rest is the soil of revelation.

Looking to Jesus, God's finished works were progressively revealed to them. For He had promised, 'On this rock I will build My church, and the gates of Hades shall not prevail against it' (Matthew 16:18). The revelation of Jesus Christ is the rock on which this church is built: 'And being assembled together with them, He [Jesus] commanded them not to depart from Jerusalem, but to wait for the Promise of the Father, 'which,' He said, 'you have heard from Me; for John truly baptised with water, but you shall be baptised with the Holy Spirit not many days from now' (Acts 1:4,5). Before they preached, taught, and healed, they were to wait on God for the promised Holy Spirit, without whom they would be impotent. They rested in God, and there, in the place of holy rest and revelation they were anointed, filled, and empowered by the Holy Spirit. They were still, they listened, they obeyed, and the Lord grew His church.

At the heart of this was the Breaking of Bread, by which the first believers were nurtured and nourished by Christ, the bread of life (John 6:41-58; 7:37-38). In the Breaking of Bread, they remembered with joy the sacrifice of the cross that made possible their restoration to fellowship with God and their receipt of life eternal! This emphasis on fellowship with Him was for every part of life. These Spirit-filled believers sought to walk in the Spirit, following His guidance in all things. Obviously, this included the leadership of church meetings. Those who led the Breaking of Bread service looked to God to guide them in it, moment by moment. This meant that although each service contained the same elements, it would also be unique, the Holy Spirit guiding leaders in their directing of the service. Like the whole of a believer's life, the Breaking of Bread service was to be a living expression of God.

As well as containing the reconstructed Breaking of Bread celebration, this book also includes an expanded version of the service containing additional introductions and explanations of its first-century use. We recommend that this version is used where people are not yet familiar with the order, or are being introduced to it for the first time. There is also a section on using this service today, which we hope will be particularly valuable to those who are unused to leading such services but who wish to celebrate as did the first believers. This is a service that anyone can follow in their own home.

As the first home of the church, Jerusalem has attracted Christian pilgrims from the first century on (Walker, 2004). 'Who would not want to worship where Christ had stood, walked, bled, and rose?' (Ruth, Steenwyk & Witvliet, 2010). We may not all be able to visit Jerusalem, but in returning to the Breaking of Bread, Jerusalem comes to us!

THE BREAKING OF BREAD SERVICE

IN THE FIRST CHURCH OF JERUSALEM

A reconstruction of the order followed by the Jerusalem Church from its inception to the siege of Jerusalem in A.D.70

PREPARATION

Those attending prepare their hearts through remembrance of the Cross, repentance and forgiveness, to share in the body and blood of Christ.

The place and the meal are prepared, with bread and wine ready.

ARRIVALS AND GREETINGS

As people arrive they greet one another, sharing the peace of God.

THE FELLOWSHIP MEAL

People take their places for the fellowship meal, and a member of the community gives thanks to God:

The Blessing Before the Meal

HA-MOTZI

Leader: BLESSED ARE YOU, O LORD OUR GOD, KING OF THE UNIVERSE, WHO BRINGS FORTH BREAD FROM THE EARTH.

All: AMEN.

The Agape meal is served.

Following the meal, when all have finished eating, a member of the community gives thanks for all God's nurture:

The Blessing After the Meal

BIRKAT HA-MAZON

Leader: BLESSED ARE YOU, O LORD OUR GOD, KING OF THE UNIVERSE, WHO NOURISHES THE WHOLE WORLD IN GOODNESS, MERCY, AND COMPASSION.

All: AMEN.

The dishes are gathered up so that the service may commence.

WELCOME AND ANNOUNCEMENTS

After the meal everyone is welcomed and necessary announcements of information and events in the life of the church are made. The leader, host, or another representative of the community, introduces the service, either in their own words, or using a welcome such as the following:

Leader: Welcome, brothers and sisters, to this celebration of Breaking of Bread given us by Jesus!

Just before His crucifixion, Jesus celebrated the Last Supper with His disciples, giving instructions that from then on we were to take bread and wine in memory of Him. At the Cross, Jesus our Messiah, the Son of God, took all our sin upon Himself, making a way for us to be reconciled to God and live in loving relationship with Him forever, walking and talking with Him each day. Sin separated us from God, but He loved us so much that He sent His Son to die in our place, bearing our sin and paying the penalty we deserved, so that we might be forgiven and become His sons and daughters.

If there are unbelievers present:

Leader: If you have accepted Jesus as your Saviour, you are welcome to share in the bread and wine here today, but if you have not yet accepted Him, and you would like to, please raise your hand now and we will pray together, and in believing you will be saved. Repeat these words after me. We will all pray the prayer together:

Heavenly Father, / I know I am a sinner, / and I am sorry for my sins. / I ask that You forgive me, / wash me and cleanse me, / from all unrighteousness. / I believe that Jesus / died for my sins / and rose from the dead. / Jesus said / that whoever / believes in Him / should not perish / but have / everlasting life. / So I believe in my heart / that Jesus died for my sins / and I believe / that God raised Him / from the dead / and He is alive. / I accept / Jesus Christ, / the risen Saviour / as my Lord / and my master. / I will do my best / to live for Him, / to serve Him, / and to walk together with Him, / all the days of my life. / And according to His promise, / I am washed, / I am cleansed, / I am justified, / I am saved.

Welcome to the Kingdom of God and to this Fellowship!

Announcements and notices are given.

The leader gives a call to worship (Heb. 'Barekhu'):

Leader: LET US PRAISE.
PRAISE THE LORD, WHO IS TO BE PRAISED!

All: PRAISED IS THE LORD, WHO IS TO BE PRAISED FOR EVER AND EVER!

Leader: PRAISED IS THE LORD, WHO IS TO BE PRAISED FOR EVER AND EVER!

One or more of the following blessings (Heb. 'Berakot') may be said:

Leader: THE LORD LIVES! AND BLESSED BE MY ROCK, AND EXALTED BE THE GOD OF THE ROCK OF MY SALVATION!

2 Samuel 22:47

All: AMEN!

Leader: BLESSED BE THE LORD GOD, THE GOD OF ISRAEL, WHO ONLY DOES WONDROUS THINGS! AND BLESSED BE HIS GLORIOUS NAME FOREVER! AND LET THE WHOLE EARTH BE FILLED WITH HIS GLORY.

Psalm 72:18,19

All: AMEN AND AMEN!

Leader: BLESSED BE THE LORD GOD OF ISRAEL FROM EVERLASTING TO EVERLASTING!

1 Chronicles 16:36

All: AMEN!

Leader: BLESSED BE THE LORD GOD OF ISRAEL, WHO MADE HEAVEN AND EARTH.

2 Chronicles 2:12

All: AMEN!

Leader: BLESSED BE YOUR GLORIOUS NAME, WHICH IS EXALTED ABOVE ALL BLESSING AND PRAISE!

Nehemiah 9:5

All: AMEN!

Leader: BLESSED BE THE LORD, BECAUSE HE HAS HEARD THE VOICE OF MY SUPPLICATIONS!

Psalm 28:6

All: AMEN!

Leader: BLESSED BE THE LORD, WHO DAILY LOADS US WITH BENEFITS, THE GOD OF OUR SALVATION!

Psalm 68:19

All: AMEN!

Leader: BLESSED IS THE NAME OF THE LORD, NOW AND FOREVER.

Psalm 113:2

All: AMEN!

Leader: BLESSED IS THE GLORY OF THE LORD FROM HIS PLACE!

Ezekiel 3:12

All: AMEN!

Leader: BLESSED BE THE NAME OF GOD FOREVER AND EVER, FOR WISDOM AND MIGHT ARE HIS.

Daniel 2:20

All: AMEN!

An opening hymn or psalm of praise may be sung.

PRAYERS

All: OUR FATHER,
WHO IS IN HEAVEN,
HALLOWED BE YOUR NAME,
YOUR KINGDOM COME,
YOUR WILL BE DONE,
ON EARTH, AS IT IS IN HEAVEN.
GIVE US THIS DAY OUR DAILY BREAD.
AND FORGIVE US OUR SINS,
AS WE FORGIVE THOSE WHO SIN AGAINST US.
AND LEAD US NOT INTO TEMPTATION,
BUT DELIVER US FROM THE EVIL ONE.
FOR YOURS IS THE KINGDOM,
THE POWER AND THE GLORY,
FOR EVER AND EVER.
AMEN.

From Matthew 6:9-13, Luke 11:2-4

A prayer for the salvation of all may be said, either extemporaneously, or using the following example:

Leader: REMEMBER IN YOUR MERCY, O GOD OUR SAVIOUR, ALL KINGS AND ALL THAT ARE IN AUTHORITY, THAT WE MAY LEAD A QUIET AND PEACEABLE LIFE IN ALL GODLINESS AND REVERENCE, FOR THIS IS GOOD AND ACCEPTABLE IN YOUR SIGHT.

All: BLESSED ARE YOU, LORD, WHO MAKES PEACE.

Leader: REMEMBER IN YOUR MERCY, O GOD OUR SAVIOUR, ALL THOSE WHOM YOU HAVE CREATED, WHETHER ALIVE IN THE BODY, OR DEPARTED THIS LIFE. WE PRAY FOR ALL, THAT YOU WILL VISIT AND HAVE MERCY UPON EACH ONE, YOU WHO DESIRE ALL TO BE SAVED AND TO COME TO THE KNOWLEDGE OF THE TRUTH. FOR THERE IS ONE GOD, AND ONE MEDIATOR BETWEEN GOD AND MEN, THE MAN CHRIST JESUS WHO GAVE HIMSELF A RANSOM FOR US ALL.

All: BLESSED ARE YOU, LORD, WHO MAKES THE DEAD ALIVE.

Leader: REMEMBER IN YOUR MERCY, O GOD OUR SAVIOUR, WE WHO CALL TO YOU NOW, THAT YOU WOULD VISIT US AND THOSE KNOWN TO US WHO ARE SUFFERING AT THIS TIME, THAT THROUGH THE MERITS OF YOUR CROSS WE MIGHT RECEIVE HEALING FROM SICKNESS, DELIVERANCE FROM AFFLICTION, AND GRACE TO HELP IN TIME OF NEED.

All: BLESSED ARE YOU, LORD, WHO HEARS PRAYER.

THE OFFERING FOR THE POOR

People come forward to the front and place their offering in the box or bag provided.

STATEMENT OF FAITH

All: CHRIST DIED FOR OUR SINS
IN ACCORDANCE WITH THE SCRIPTURES,
HE WAS BURIED,
AND HE WAS RAISED ON THE THIRD DAY
IN ACCORDANCE WITH THE SCRIPTURES.
HALLELUIA!

From 1 Corinthians 15:3,4

PSALMS, HYMNS AND SPIRITUAL SONGS

One or more psalms, hymns or choruses may be sung.

SINGING IN TONGUES

Those gathered unite in praise and worship to God, singing in the Spirit.

A TIME OF HOLY SILENCE AND LISTENING TO GOD

A minute's silence is held, listening to God in stillness and silence.

REVELATION BY THE HOLY SPIRIT

Believers share what they have received from the Lord through words of wisdom or knowledge, tongues with interpretation, or through prophecy.

THE CRY OF THE SERAPHIM

All: HOLY, HOLY, HOLY IS THE LORD OF HOSTS;
THE WHOLE EARTH IS FULL OF HIS GLORY!

Isaiah 6:3

A song or hymn of God's holiness may be sung.

THE READING FROM THE HOLY GOSPEL

(STORIES OF CHRIST'S MINISTRY)

Reader: A READING FROM THE GOSPEL OF (BOOK), CHAPTER (N.), STARTING AT VERSE (N.)

The reader reads the Gospel text for the day, as given in the calendar of daily scripture readings throughout the year (Appendix A). Any member of the congregation may read. There may be one or more readers, who are invited to read by the leader.

THE APOSTLES' TEACHING

Reader: A READING FROM (BOOK), CHAPTER (N.), STARTING AT VERSE (N.)

The reader reads the additional New Testament reading for the day, as given in the calendar of daily scripture readings throughout the year (Appendix A). Any member of the congregation may read. There may be one or more readers, who are invited to read by the leader.

ONE OR MORE MESSAGES

Any members of the church who are moved by the Lord to share a brief word of encouragement or insight may now do so. These should be short and the speakers no more than three in number. The main speaker then brings the message he or she has prepared and concludes by praying for those gathered.

REPENTANCE

A moment of silent reflection and repentance.

PRAYERS OF HEALING & CONSECRATION

There may be prayers for specific needs, including prayer for healing and deliverance. Here there may also be the consecration of individuals to tasks, missions, roles and ministries.

THANKSGIVING

Believers take turns in giving thanks to God for the Cross.

A song or hymn on the message of the Cross or on the blood of Jesus may be sung.

THE BREAKING OF BREAD

The leader reads the words of institution spoken by Our Lord and Saviour at the Last Supper on the night in which He was betrayed.

Leader: THE LORD JESUS ON THE SAME NIGHT IN WHICH HE WAS BETRAYED TOOK BREAD; AND WHEN HE HAD GIVEN THANKS, HE BROKE IT AND SAID, 'TAKE, EAT; THIS IS MY BODY WHICH IS BROKEN FOR YOU; DO THIS IN REMEMBRANCE OF ME.'

IN THE SAME MANNER HE ALSO TOOK THE CUP AFTER SUPPER, SAYING, 'THIS CUP IS THE NEW COVENANT IN MY BLOOD. THIS DO, AS OFTEN AS YOU DRINK IT, IN REMEMBRANCE OF ME.'

The bread and wine are then distributed to all, the bread having been broken into pieces beforehand, and individual glasses or cups having been made ready.

The leader invites all those that are born again to take the bread, repeating Christ's words, 'Take eat; this is My body which is broken for you; do this in remembrance of Me.'

The leader invites all those that are born again to take the wine, repeating Christ's words, 'This cup is the cup of the New Covenant in My blood. This do, as often as you drink it, in remembrance of Me.'

Having received the bread and wine, those present open their hearts to God, asking Him to fill them afresh with His Holy Spirit.

THE BLESSING

When all those present have shared in Christ's body and blood, the leader gives the blessing:

Leader: THE LORD BLESS YOU, AND KEEP YOU.
THE LORD MAKE HIS FACE SHINE UPON YOU,
AND BE GRACIOUS TO YOU.
THE LORD LIFT UP HIS COUNTENANCE UPON YOU,
AND GIVE YOU PEACE.

Numbers 6:24-26

All: AMEN.

A concluding hymn may be sung.

After the service, pieces of the blessed bread are taken to the sick, those in prison, and any others who were prevented from attending.

THE BREAKING OF BREAD SERVICE

IN THE FIRST CHURCH OF JERUSALEM

A reconstruction of the order followed by the Jerusalem Church from its inception to the siege of Jerusalem in A.D.70

With additional directions and explanations of its first-century use

PREPARATION

Those attending prepare their hearts through remembrance of the Cross, repentance and forgiveness, to share in the body and blood of Christ.

The place and the meal are prepared, with bread and wine ready.

Leader: Our celebration today is a reconstruction of the Breaking of Bread service from the first Christian church, founded at Jerusalem in the first century A.D. Although now generally known by other names, this service was, and still is today, the central celebration of the church.

Let us begin by remembering why we are here. Before going to the Cross and dying there for us, Jesus inaugurated this unique meal in the company of His disciples at the Last Supper. Taking bread and wine with them, He commanded that this practice be kept in memory of Him. This they faithfully did, as we will do today.

Let us also pause for a moment to ensure that our hearts are right with God, and with one another. Is there something of which we need to repent? Let us bring it to Him now, and receive His full and free forgiveness. Is there anyone we need to forgive? Let us take that step of forgiveness now, in Jesus' name. Is there anyone from whom we would seek forgiveness? Let us reach out to them from our heart now, saying that we are sorry.

ARRIVALS AND GREETINGS

As people arrive they greet one another, sharing the peace of God.

Leader: When people arrived for this celebration in the first century, they would greet one another and then take their places for the fellowship meal.

THE FELLOWSHIP MEAL

People take their places for the fellowship meal, and a member of the community gives thanks to God.

Leader: In the first church, the Breaking of Bread, or Eucharist, or Holy Communion, was celebrated after a meal, just as Jesus celebrated it at the Last Supper. Before they ate, they would give thanks. Jesus always gave thanks for His food, and the church He established would have done the same. We will say the Jewish grace that He likely said. Let us give thanks:

The Blessing Before the Meal

HA-MOTZI

Leader: BLESSED ARE YOU, O LORD OUR GOD, KING OF THE UNIVERSE, WHO BRINGS FORTH BREAD FROM THE EARTH.

All: AMEN.

The Agape meal is served.

Following the meal, when all have finished eating, a member of the community gives thanks for all God's nurture.

Leader: When everyone had fully finished eating, someone would have given thanks for all God's love for the world.

The Blessing After the Meal

BIRKAT HA-MAZON

Leader: BLESSED ARE YOU, O LORD OUR GOD, KING OF THE UNIVERSE, WHO NOURISHES THE WHOLE WORLD IN GOODNESS, MERCY, AND COMPASSION.

All: AMEN.

The dishes are gathered up so that the service may commence.

Leader: Following this prayer the dishes are gathered up and the tables are cleared, so that the service may begin.

WELCOME AND ANNOUNCEMENTS

After the meal everyone is welcomed and necessary announcements of information and events in the life of the church are made. The leader, host, or another representative of the community, introduces the service, either in their own words, or using a welcome such as the following:

Leader: This is the point in the first century Breaking of Bread at which they would probably have welcomed everyone and shared announcements of events in the life of the church. A leader, host, or another representative of the community would briefly introduce the service. There would have been no set words for this, but it would probably have been similar to the following:

Welcome, brothers and sisters, to this celebration of Breaking of Bread given us by Jesus! Just before His crucifixion, Jesus celebrated the Last Supper with His disciples, giving instructions that from then on we were to take bread and wine in memory of Him. At the Cross, Jesus our Messiah, the Son of God, took all our sin upon Himself, making a way for us to be reconciled to God and live in loving relationship with Him forever, walking and talking with Him each day. Sin separated us from God, but He loved us so much that He sent His Son to die in our place, bearing our sin and paying the penalty we deserved, so that we might be forgiven and become His sons and daughters.

If there are unbelievers present:

Leader: If you have accepted Jesus as your Saviour, you are welcome to share in the bread and wine here today, but if you have not yet accepted Him, and you would like to, please raise your hand now and we will pray together, and in believing you will be saved. Repeat these words after me. We will all pray the prayer together:

Heavenly Father, / I know I am a sinner, / and I am sorry for my sins. / I ask that You forgive me, / wash me and cleanse me, / from all unrighteousness. / I believe that Jesus / died for my sins / and rose from the dead. / Jesus said / that whoever / believes in Him / should not perish / but have / everlasting life. / So I believe in my heart / that Jesus died for my sins / and I believe / that God raised Him / from the dead / and He is alive. / I accept / Jesus Christ, / the risen Saviour / as my Lord / and my master. / I will do my best / to live for Him / to serve Him / and to walk together with Him / all the days of my life. / And according to His promise, / I am washed, / I am cleansed, / I am justified, / I am saved.

Welcome to the Kingdom of God and to this Fellowship!

Announcements and notices are given.

The leader gives a call to worship (Heb. 'Barekhu').

Leader: Once the meal and the announcements were concluded the leader would probably have given the traditional Hebrew call to worship, saying:

LET US PRAISE.
PRAISE THE LORD, WHO IS TO BE PRAISED!

All: PRAISED IS THE LORD, WHO IS TO BE PRAISED FOR EVER AND EVER!

Leader: PRAISED IS THE LORD, WHO IS TO BE PRAISED FOR EVER AND EVER!

One or more of the following blessings (Heb. 'Berakot') may be said.

Leader: It is likely that the service began with an expression of praise to God. Such expressions, called 'Berakot' in Hebrew were a familiar part of worship at that time.

THE LORD LIVES! AND BLESSED BE MY ROCK, AND EXALTED BE THE GOD OF THE ROCK OF MY SALVATION!

2 Samuel 22:47

All: AMEN!

Leader: BLESSED BE THE LORD GOD, THE GOD OF ISRAEL, WHO ONLY DOES WONDROUS THINGS! AND BLESSED BE HIS GLORIOUS NAME FOREVER! AND LET THE WHOLE EARTH BE FILLED WITH HIS GLORY.

Psalm 72:18,19

All: AMEN AND AMEN!

Leader: BLESSED BE THE LORD GOD OF ISRAEL FROM EVERLASTING TO EVERLASTING!

1 Chronicles 16:36

All: AMEN!

Leader: BLESSED BE THE LORD GOD OF ISRAEL, WHO MADE HEAVEN AND EARTH.

2 Chronicles 2:12

All: AMEN!

Leader: BLESSED BE YOUR GLORIOUS NAME, WHICH IS EXALTED ABOVE ALL BLESSING AND PRAISE!

Nehemiah 9:5

All: AMEN!

Leader: BLESSED BE THE LORD, BECAUSE HE HAS HEARD THE VOICE OF MY SUPPLICATIONS!

Psalm 28:6

All: AMEN!

Leader: BLESSED BE THE LORD, WHO DAILY LOADS US WITH BENEFITS, THE GOD OF OUR SALVATION!

Psalm 68:19

All: AMEN!

Leader: BLESSED IS THE NAME OF THE LORD, NOW AND FOREVER.

Psalm 113:2

All: AMEN!

Leader: BLESSED IS THE GLORY OF THE LORD FROM HIS PLACE!

Ezekiel 3:12

All: AMEN!

Leader: BLESSED BE THE NAME OF GOD FOREVER AND EVER, FOR WISDOM AND MIGHT ARE HIS.

Daniel 2:20

All: AMEN!

An opening hymn or psalm of praise may be sung.

Leader: At this point they may well have sung a hymn of praise. We know that they sang in worship in the first century as the Jewish people had sung for centuries. We do not have any surviving scores from this period, but we do have the Book of Psalms, the hymn book of Israel, from which scroll and from memory they would have sung.

PRAYERS

Leader: The first church had a rich treasury of resources from which to draw for their meetings. This included their experience of Temple worship, their knowledge of the synagogue service held every Sabbath, and all that they remembered of Christ's earthly ministry. Jesus showed them many things, but there was one prayer in particular that He taught which would have been a part of their worship. This is the prayer we know as The Lord's Prayer. Let us say it together:

All: OUR FATHER,
WHO IS IN HEAVEN,
HALLOWED BE YOUR NAME,
YOUR KINGDOM COME,
YOUR WILL BE DONE,
ON EARTH, AS IT IS IN HEAVEN.
GIVE US THIS DAY OUR DAILY BREAD.
AND FORGIVE US OUR SINS,
AS WE FORGIVE THOSE WHO SIN AGAINST US.
AND LEAD US NOT INTO TEMPTATION,
BUT DELIVER US FROM THE EVIL ONE.
FOR YOURS IS THE KINGDOM,
THE POWER AND THE GLORY,
FOR EVER AND EVER.
AMEN.

From Matthew 6:9-13, Luke 11:2-4

A prayer for the salvation of all may be said, either extemporaneously, or using the following example.

Leader: We know from Paul's letter to Timothy that the first believers prayed for people everywhere, including those in authority, and those in need. It is unlikely that there was a fixed form for this prayer at the beginning. Believers would have prayed in their own words. The following is an example of the kind of prayer that might have been said. Let us pray for all:

REMEMBER IN YOUR MERCY, O GOD OUR SAVIOUR, ALL KINGS AND ALL THAT ARE IN AUTHORITY, THAT WE MAY LEAD A QUIET AND PEACEABLE LIFE IN ALL GODLINESS AND REVERENCE, FOR THIS IS GOOD AND ACCEPTABLE IN YOUR SIGHT.

All: BLESSED ARE YOU, LORD, WHO MAKES PEACE.

Leader: REMEMBER IN YOUR MERCY, O GOD OUR SAVIOUR, ALL THOSE WHOM YOU HAVE CREATED, WHETHER ALIVE IN THE BODY, OR DEPARTED THIS LIFE. WE PRAY FOR ALL, THAT YOU WILL VISIT AND HAVE MERCY UPON EACH ONE, YOU WHO DESIRE ALL TO BE SAVED AND TO COME TO THE KNOWLEDGE OF THE TRUTH. FOR THERE IS ONE GOD, AND ONE MEDIATOR BETWEEN GOD AND MEN, THE MAN CHRIST JESUS WHO GAVE HIMSELF A RANSOM FOR US ALL.

All: BLESSED ARE YOU, LORD, WHO MAKES THE DEAD ALIVE.

Leader: REMEMBER IN YOUR MERCY, O GOD OUR SAVIOUR, WE WHO CALL TO YOU NOW, THAT YOU WOULD VISIT US AND THOSE KNOWN TO US WHO ARE SUFFERING AT THIS TIME, THAT THROUGH THE MERITS OF YOUR CROSS WE MIGHT RECEIVE HEALING FROM SICKNESS, DELIVERANCE FROM AFFLICTION, AND GRACE TO HELP IN TIME OF NEED.

All: BLESSED ARE YOU, LORD, WHO HEARS PRAYER.

THE OFFERING FOR THE POOR

People come forward to the front and place their offering in the box or bag provided.

Leader: It would have been natural at this point, when everyone was thinking about the needs of others, for the first believers to take up their offering. There was no pressure to give in the first church, but being moved by love and compassion, people wanted to give what they could for the support of the poor. The first church had no paid ministers, so most, if not all, of what was given went to help those in need. The same is true today for all those who fully represent the first church.

Let us bring our offerings to the LORD, for the support of the poor and the alleviation of their suffering.

STATEMENT OF FAITH

Leader: An important moment in the first Breaking of Bread services would have been the proclamation of their faith. They did not have the creeds that are familiar to us, for these were developed centuries later. But they did have a creed, which is found in our New Testament, and which perfectly expresses the heart of our faith.

Let us boldly proclaim our faith:

All: CHRIST DIED FOR OUR SINS
IN ACCORDANCE WITH THE SCRIPTURES,
HE WAS BURIED,
AND HE WAS RAISED ON THE THIRD DAY
IN ACCORDANCE WITH THE SCRIPTURES.
HALLELUIA!

From 1 Corinthians 15:3,4

PSALMS, HYMNS AND SPIRITUAL SONGS

One or more psalms, hymns or choruses may be sung.

Leader: We know that this first Christian community sang, sometimes no doubt with musical instruments. The last hymn in their songbook, Psalm 150, encourages us to praise the LORD with every instrument and with every breath. First century instruments would have included the trumpet, the lute, the harp, the timbrel, stringed instruments, flutes, and cymbals.

SINGING IN TONGUES

Those gathered unite in praise and worship to God, singing in the Spirit.

Leader: For the first believers, worship in song would have naturally led into singing in the Spirit. The first church received the outpouring of the Holy Spirit on the Day of Pentecost and speaking in tongues not known by the speaker was the first manifestation. This would have been a natural moment in the service to sing out in heavenly worship, singing the songs of the angels. If you have never sung in the spirit, it is very easy. Just start singing out to God, letting words form as you do.

Let us sing that last song again, and then lift up our hearts and voices to God, singing in the Spirit.

A TIME OF HOLY SILENCE AND LISTENING TO GOD

A minute's silence is held, listening to God in stillness and silence.

Leader: When the song of the Spirit ends, there is often a profound and living silence, for we have as it were, entered within the veil, and we stand in the Holy Place, the Throne Room of God. It is fitting that having come to this place, every tongue falls silent, and we listen to hear what He would say to us.

Let us be still and silent in our hearts as we listen to whatever the LORD would say to us personally. Imagine that He is with you, for indeed He is. What do you hear Him say?

[A minute's silence]

Whatever we have just received from God we ought to take to heart, for His words to us will be by far the most important words we hear in this life. Consider keeping a journal in which you record His word to you each day. Jesus said, 'My sheep know My voice,' and this is important because there are many voices that speak in the human mind, including those of the demons who will try to deceive us. Do not allow this fact to stop you listening to God, but persevere in seeking Him, listening to Him each day, and in time your spiritual senses will become trained through practice to discern between good and evil.

REVELATION BY THE HOLY SPIRIT

Believers share what they have received from the Lord.

Leader: Let us hear whatever the Lord would reveal to us, whether through words of wisdom or knowledge, through tongues with interpretation, or through prophecy.

THE CRY OF THE SERAPHIM

A song or hymn of God's holiness may be sung.

Leader: Having drawn near to God and heard from heaven, what could be more appropriate than to say or sing the 'thrice-holy hymn, the earliest form of which, found in the book of the prophet Isaiah, would have been familiar to the Jewish worshippers of the first century.

All: HOLY, HOLY, HOLY IS THE LORD OF HOSTS;
THE WHOLE EARTH IS FULL OF HIS GLORY!

Isaiah 6:3

THE READING FROM THE HOLY GOSPEL

(STORIES OF CHRIST'S MINISTRY)

Reader: A READING FROM THE GOSPEL OF (BOOK), CHAPTER (N.), STARTING AT VERSE (N.)

The reader reads the Gospel text for the day, as given in the calendar of daily scripture readings throughout the year (Appendix A). Any member of the congregation may read. There may be one or more readers, who are invited to read by the leader.

Leader: Some of the resources we have in the church today did not exist at the inception of the first church, and this includes the four written gospel accounts at the start of our New Testament. Whether we support an earlier or a later date for the authorship of the gospels, we must acknowledge that they were not there at the beginning. No one had a New Testament, because it had not yet been written.

But they had something we do not have: the eye witness testimony of the apostles, and not just the apostles. There were many who could tell their stories about Jesus. When they came together, people would have told these stories, encouraging and building up the church.

It is a proof of the authenticity of the gospel accounts that there were so many witnesses, making it impossible for an erroneous account to find acceptance amongst believers. Fewer witnesses might have made it easier to falsify the truth, but with multitudes having witnessed His ministry such fabrication was impossible. We can trust the gospels.

THE APOSTLES' TEACHING

Reader: A READING FROM (BOOK), CHAPTER (N.), STARTING AT VERSE (N.)

The reader reads the additional New Testament reading for the day, as given in the calendar of daily scripture readings throughout the year (Appendix A). Any member of the congregation may read. There may be one or more readers, who are invited to read by the leader.

Leader: Just as the four gospels had not yet been written when the Jerusalem church began, so also the remainder of our New Testament had yet to be penned. But again, the apostles were there, bringing their teaching in person. Today we have a New Testament full of inspired writings, mostly from the second half of the first century. We cannot listen to the apostles in person as they did, but we can hear their messages ringing out across the centuries from the wonderful texts they wrote.

ONE OR MORE MESSAGES

Any members of the church who are moved by the Lord to share a brief word of encouragement or insight may now do so. These should be short and the speakers no more than three in number. The main speaker then brings the message he or she has prepared and concludes by praying for those gathered.

Leader: Just as in the synagogue of that day, it was usual for a number of people to share an insight or message. There would have been a limit on this, with most people sharing fairly briefly. The main speaker would take a little longer.

REPENTANCE

A moment of silent reflection and repentance.

Leader: Let us examine our hearts and our lives, confessing our sins to Almighty God in silent prayer, and turning from them in repentance and faith.

PRAYERS OF HEALING & CONSECRATION

A time of prayer for those in need, including prayer for healing and deliverance. Here there may also be the consecration of individuals to tasks, missions, roles and ministries.

Leader: Just as today, sometimes there would have been specific matters needing prayer, such as prayer for healing if there were any sick amongst them, or prayers of consecration if there was a need to appoint people to specific roles in the fellowship.

THANKSGIVING

Believers take turns in giving thanks to God for the Cross.

Leader: Let us give thanks to God for the sacrifice of the Cross and the new life we have thereby received.

A song or hymn on the message of the Cross or on the blood of Jesus may be sung.

THE BREAKING OF BREAD

Leader: We now come to the heart of our service, the breaking of bread in memory of our Saviour. Like Jesus and the twelve, we began our celebration with a meal of friendship and fellowship, and now we follow it by sharing in His body and blood. At this point the leader would remind everyone of Jesus' words at the Last Supper when He established the practice of taking bread and wine in this way.

The leader reads the words of institution spoken by Our Lord and Saviour at the Last Supper on the night in which He was betrayed.

Leader: THE LORD JESUS ON THE SAME NIGHT IN WHICH HE WAS BETRAYED TOOK BREAD; AND WHEN HE HAD GIVEN THANKS, HE BROKE IT AND SAID, 'TAKE, EAT; THIS IS MY BODY WHICH IS BROKEN FOR YOU; DO THIS IN REMEMBRANCE OF ME.'

IN THE SAME MANNER HE ALSO TOOK THE CUP AFTER SUPPER, SAYING, 'THIS CUP IS THE NEW COVENANT IN MY BLOOD. THIS DO, AS OFTEN AS YOU DRINK IT, IN REMEMBRANCE OF ME.'

The bread and wine are then distributed to all, the bread having been broken into pieces beforehand, and individual glasses or cups having been made ready.

The leader invites all those that are born again to take the bread, repeating Christ's words, 'Take eat; this is My body which is broken for you; do this in remembrance of Me.'

The leader invites all those that are born again to take the wine, repeating Christ's words, 'This cup is the cup of the New Covenant in My blood. This do, as often as you drink it, in remembrance of Me.'

Having received the bread and wine, those present open their hearts to God, asking Him to fill them afresh with His Holy Spirit.

THE BLESSING

When all those present have shared in Christ's body and blood, the leader gives the blessing.

Leader: When everyone has taken the bread and the wine, the service concludes with the blessing that God's people had used for centuries. This blessing was given by God Himself, when He spoke to Moses saying, 'Speak to Aaron and his sons, saying, "This is the way you shall bless the children of Israel."' This blessing is recorded in the Bible, in the book of Numbers, chapter 6, verses 22 to 26.

THE LORD BLESS YOU, AND KEEP YOU.
THE LORD MAKE HIS FACE SHINE UPON YOU,
AND BE GRACIOUS TO YOU.
THE LORD LIFT UP HIS COUNTENANCE UPON YOU,
AND GIVE YOU PEACE.

Numbers 6:24-26

All: AMEN.

A concluding hymn may be sung.

Leader: It is not unlikely that just as at the Last Supper, this joyful gathering concluded with a final hymn or song of praise.

After the service, pieces of the blessed bread are taken to the sick, those in prison, and any others who were prevented from attending the service.

THE RECONSTRUCTION

And they continued steadfastly in the apostles' teaching and fellowship, in the breaking of bread, and in prayers.

Acts 2:42

Have you ever wondered what it might have been like to attend one of the first celebrations of the Eucharist in the early church? Many have, and it is hoped that through this revival of the first Liturgy, Mass or Holy Communion, believers may experience the heart of early Christianity and enjoy a fresh spiritual outpouring of apostolic life and health through the blessed Holy Spirit.

The order of service presented here represents a speculative reconstruction of the Breaking of Bread celebration in the first Christian church. Up to the present day, no first century document has been discovered detailing the components of this service and their order. Our earliest surviving documentary records of Christian liturgy appear to date from the 4th century A.D., although it may still be said today, as Palmer stated over a century ago, that, 'The period when liturgies were first committed to writing is uncertain, and has been the subject of some controversy' (Palmer, 1832). By the time these orders were written down, it is likely that many changes would have been made to the original order, changes that included the removal of the fellowship meal.

Thankfully there is evidence, found largely in the New Testament text, upon which we can draw in the reconstruction of this seminal event, and it is largely to these that the service here presented owes its form. We do not claim that this is the only valid reconstruction possible, but that it is a plausible one, given the information we have at the present time. Other reconstructions are possible (e.g. Messmer, 2019) as the evidence permits a variety of interpretations.

The Breaking of Bread service was as much the central service of the first church as it has been the central service of the church in every age. This was the clear intention of its initiator, the Lord Jesus Christ, who at the Last Supper inaugurated the practice of taking bread and wine in His memory. Following the example of our founder, the first church continued this practice in the context of an evening meal. This was their custom, not only at Jerusalem but wherever a new church was formed. Writing to the church at Corinth, around twenty years after the inception of the church at Jerusalem, the apostle Paul refers to this service using terms that denote both a gathering and a meal (1 Corinthians 11:17-34). The original context of the Eucharist was thus a fellowship meal and this was normative for the church of the first century.

This conjunction of activities would not have seemed strange to people in first-century Israel. The combination of a meal with a specific time for discussion afterwards was not uncommon in the Greco-Roman world of the first century, and the significance of this 'Greco-Roman banquet' for the origins of early Christian liturgy has been considered by a number of modern liturgiologists (Smith, 2003; Alikin, 2010; Bradshaw & Johnson, 2012; McGowan, 2014). As enjoyed in the wider culture, this event was in two parts. The first consisted of a meal, whilst the second took the form of a symposium, typically including discussion and entertainment.

Luke records that the Breaking of Bread took place in houses (Acts 2:46) on the first day of the week (Acts 20:7; 1 Corinthians 16:2), which was the day of Christ's resurrection (John 20:1; Revelation 1:10). From the beginning, Sunday was the main day on which Christian believers met, and on this day they commemorated Christ's atoning work, pre-eminently in the breaking of bread, which as we have seen was an evening meal. However, this meal did not take place on Sunday evening, for the first century reckoning of the day placed the start of the day at sunset. Consequently, the first day of the week began at sunset on the Sabbath, which means that breaking of bread generally took place on Saturday evening. After sunset on the Sabbath, Christian believers, who at the start were mostly if not wholly Jewish, would gather in homes to celebrate together the greatest banquet of our age.

This is not to say that the Breaking of Bread did not also take place at other times. In obeying Jesus' command at the Last Supper to do this in His memory, believers were free to break bread at any time, which they no doubt did, some even daily. There have been many in the history of the church whose desire to know Christ has been expressed in breaking bread each day. Notable amongst these was the modern day apostle Smith Wigglesworth, who is reported to have raised 14 people from the dead. Wigglesworth, 'did this every day whether he was at home or not. If other believers were with him, he would share with them. If not, he would partake alone' (Stormont, 1989). For those who wish to break bread at the start of each day, an order for personal communion is included in Appendix B.

Believing that it is possible to identify the likely components of the first century Eucharistic meal, we have endeavoured to construct what we hope is a close approximation to what took place. But whilst we may have some confidence in the components themselves, the same may not be said of their order. In this reconstruction we have sought to place the components in the order we think most likely, given what we learn from the New Testament text, and informed by what we know of first century Jewish culture and worship.

It is possible, indeed likely, that at this early point in the development of the church, the order was not entirely fixed, but rather flexible, allowing for some variation. It is likely that certain components would have been present in every celebration, and that some of these, such as the Lord's Prayer, as well as the formula given by Christ for the institution and administration of the bread and wine, would have had much the same wording wherever used. At the same time, it appears that there was likely a high degree of extemporisation, participants expressing prayer, praise, and teaching largely in their own words (1 Corinthians 14:26). This was similar to the services of the first century synagogues, where participants made extemporary contributions within an overall structure familiar to all. Thus the first communion celebrations were unscripted, containing both fixed and variable elements. There was a pattern to their services, but no single order that was followed in exactly the same way on every occasion. We have sought to create a 'representative' service, which believers may take and use in a flexible and creative way under the guidance of the Holy Spirit, as we believe they did at the beginning.

The order we have chosen is as follows:

1 Preparation
2 Arrivals and greetings
3 The fellowship meal
4 Welcome and announcements
5 Prayers
6 The offering for the poor
7 Statement of faith
8 Psalms, hymns and spiritual songs
9 Singing in tongues
10 Holy silence and listening to God
11 Revelation by the Holy Spirit
12 The cry of the seraphim (The thrice-holy hymn)
13 Stories of Christ's ministry (A reading from the Gospels)
14 The apostles' teaching (An additional reading from the New Testament)
15 One or more messages
16 Repentance
17 Prayers of healing and consecration
18 Thanksgiving
19 The breaking of bread
20 The blessing
21 Closing hymn

There may be some who are surprised at the relative sophistication of this order. To expect the initial structure and practices of an organised society to be simpler than its later expressions may be reasonable, but we must not discount the fact that the church received rich resources at her inception. Firstly, Christ had Himself spent three years preparing its leaders for their future work, providing them with both a powerful role model for ministry and a cultural model of how things were to be done amongst believers. Secondly, the first church was built primarily on revelation, ensuring that the intelligence and sophistication of its initial structure transcended that which might be built by human means alone. Thirdly, the first leaders were Jews who brought with them the influence of their history and tradition, with a new and deeper understanding of that inheritance received from the teaching of their Jewish Lord, Master, and Messiah. The first Christian church, born of the Father, built by Christ, and empowered by the Holy Spirit, stood on the foundation of Abraham, Moses and the Prophets, inheriting many centuries of truth and wisdom. Thus, it could only be called 'primitive' in the narrow technical sense of its chronological position as the first ekklesia. In every other respect this church, founded by Christ Himself, represented the most advanced expression of religious fellowship ever seen on earth.

Worship in the first church was highly participatory, with every worshipper entitled to contribute in some way that would build up those present (1 Corinthians 14:26). This contribution could be a song or a hymn, teaching or encouragement, insight or revelation, a message in their own language or in a tongue not known by the speaker, an interpretation of tongues, prophecy, or some other appropriate offering. There were guidelines for participation to ensure order, such as are reiterated by Paul in his correspondence with the church at Corinth (1 Corinthians 14:27-33).

Freedom of participation followed naturally from their understanding of a common priesthood, most clearly stated by

Peter in 1 Peter 2:5-9, and affirmed many years later by the apostle John in the book of Revelation (Revelation 1:6; 5:10). Through Christ's atoning sacrifice all believers now had access to God without the need for any other priestly intermediary. In the first church, every believer is a priest, and every home a church.

Numbers attending services were not large by today's standards, being limited by the size of homes available for use. Archaeological excavations of wealthy Roman homes suggest that around nine diners could be accommodated reclining at tables, or double that number if seated, as seems to have been the case (cf. 1 Corinthians 14:30; James 2:2,3). If the atrium area of a Roman villa was used, around forty to fifty people could be accommodated. The church grew rapidly, requiring the continual addition of homes serving as venues for the breaking of bread.

(1) PREPARATION

Those attending prepare their hearts through remembrance of the Cross, repentance and forgiveness, to share in the body and blood of Christ.

The place is prepared, with bread and wine ready.

Preparation for the breaking of bread was and is both personal and practical. Personal preparation involves self-examination that we might eat the bread and drink the wine in a worthy manner. We prepare our hearts, which begins with remembering why we are breaking bread. We recall how before He went to the Cross and died there in our place, Jesus inaugurated this unique meal with His disciples. Taking bread and wine, He shared them with His disciples, commanding them to keep this practice in memory of Him. We are fulfilling His commandment.

Our personal preparation is pre-eminently a time for repentance. Lying at the heart of Old Testament life, the necessity of personal repentance was never lost during the transition to the

Messianic synagogue. John preached repentance, as did Christ, as well as the apostles sent out in His name. Understanding that the Lord desires a pure offering (Malachi 1:11,14), the leaders of the first church would have maintained the primacy of repentance. In the same vein, Paul emphasises the place of confession and repentance in the Eucharist, as preparatory to the communion itself, suggesting that this was their practice from the beginning: 'Whoever eats this bread or drinks this cup of the Lord in an unworthy manner will be guilty of the body and blood of the Lord. But let a man examine himself, and so let him eat of the bread and drink of the cup. For he who eats and drinks in an unworthy manner eats and drinks judgement to himself, not discerning the Lord's body. For this reason, many are weak and sick among you, and many are dead. For if we would judge ourselves, we would not be judged. But when we are judged, we are chastened by the Lord, that we may not be condemned with the world' (1 Corinthians 11:27-32).

Thus we make our hearts right with God and with one another. Is there something of which we need to repent? Is there anyone we need to forgive? Is there anyone from whom we would seek forgiveness? Through self-examination we remember our wrongdoing, judging ourselves in our attitudes, thoughts, motives, emotions and actions. We are particularly concerned to examine our love for God and our neighbour. To what degree have we loved, trusted, and walked with the Lord? And to what degree have we acted in love and compassion towards others? Coming before Him in repentance, we receive His forgiveness by faith, and we extend our forgiveness to those who have sinned against us.

Preparation is also practical. Just as the Last Supper required that a place and provisions be prepared (Matthew 26:17-19), so the Breaking of Bread, or Lord's Supper, requires similar preparation. Firstly, a suitable place must be chosen, and in the first century this would have been a home. For the first few centuries there were no church buildings so the church met in homes (Acts 12:12; Romans

16:5,23; Colossians 4:14; Philemon 1-4), the Temple (Acts 5:12), public auditoriums of schools (Acts 19:9), and in synagogues whilst they were permitted to (Acts 14:1,3; 17:1; 18:4). Meeting together often meant going to a home, or, having people come to your home, in order to worship. Every Christian home was a place of worship and a place where people could break bread. As E.E. Cairns points out, 'The early Christians did not think of a church as a place of worship according to the common usage of the word today. A church signified a body of people in personal relationship with Christ' (Cairns, 1981).

Secondly, a meal must also be ordered or prepared, however simple this meal might be. Thirdly, and most important of all, bread and wine must be made ready.

(2) ARRIVALS AND GREETINGS

As people arrive they greet one another, sharing the peace of God.

Imagine that people are arriving at the home. As they arrive they greet one another. In the first century this took the form of a 'holy kiss'. Three scriptures reveal that the Eucharistic services of the first church contained a Kiss of Peace (1 Corinthians 16:20, 2 Corinthians 13:12, 1 Thessalonians 5:26). This was a non-sexual blessing exchanged by persons of the same gender.

(3) THE FELLOWSHIP MEAL

People take their places for the fellowship meal, and a member of the community gives thanks to God.

On arrival, people took their places for the fellowship meal. Following Jesus' example at the last supper, the first believers met together for a communal meal, the 'Agape' or 'Love Feast' (Jude 1:12), where they ate together before sharing bread and wine in memory of Him. Not only did our Lord choose to commemorate

His atoning sacrifice with the eating of bread and drinking of wine, but He also set this act of remembrance within the context of a shared meal, His object lesson illustrating through its Divine association the symbiotic relationship between heavenly and earthly fellowship. As He had so often eaten together with others in life, so now He ate with them in His death and resurrection. In the words of C.H. Spurgeon, 'Communion is strength, solitude is weakness. Alone, the fine old beech yields to the blast, and lies prone upon the sward; in the forest, supporting each other, the trees laugh at the hurricane. The sheep of Jesus flock together; the social element is the genius of Christianity' (Spurgeon, 1870).

The meal would have commenced with a blessing. It was Jesus' custom to give thanks before eating (see Matthew 15:36). The ancient rabbis taught that we have an obligation to acknowledge that all the fruits of the earth are a gift from God (Psalm 24:1), and to give thanks when partaking of any of them. Jesus likely spoke the traditional Jewish form of blessing before the meal, known as the Ha-Motzi. This would have been the opening benediction at the Agape meal, 'bread' being a symbol of all food:

The Blessing Before the Meal

HA-MOTZI

Leader: BLESSED ARE YOU, O LORD OUR GOD, KING OF THE UNIVERSE, WHO BRINGS FORTH BREAD FROM THE EARTH.

All: AMEN.

The Agape meal is served.

Following the meal, when all have finished eating, a member of the community gives thanks for all God's nurture.

When everyone had fully finished eating, someone would have given thanks for all God's love for the world. The Birkat Ha-Mazon blessing, or Grace after Meals, is a Biblical commandment (Deuteronomy 8:10). Jesus and the apostles would have been familiar with Birkat Ha-Mazon and it is likely that at least some sort of abridged form would conclude a communal meal. It's three benedictions are among the most ancient Jewish prayers and their general content is thought to go back to at least the days of the Maccabees. Josephus dates the text of Birkat Ha-Mazon to at least the time of Simon ben Shetah, about 100 B.C. It is likely that a three paragraph version was already in existence by the time of the destruction of the Temple and if so, this may have been used at the Agape. Alternatively, they may have used the more ancient form, now lost to us. The following reconstruction of this initial form, based upon comparisons of early variants of the text, is that of Finkelstein (1929), and it is this version that we follow:

The Blessing After the Meal

BIRKAT HA-MAZON

Leader: BLESSED ARE YOU, O LORD OUR GOD, KING OF THE UNIVERSE, WHO NOURISHES THE WHOLE WORLD IN GOODNESS, MERCY, AND COMPASSION.

All: AMEN.

The dishes are gathered up and the tables cleared, so that the service may commence.

(4) WELCOME AND ANNOUNCEMENTS

> *After the meal everyone is welcomed and necessary announcements of information and events in the life of the church are made. The leader, host, or another representative of the community, introduces the service.*

This welcome would most likely have been given by a representative of the community, perhaps an apostle, or by the leader of the church in that house, the latter's role likely being equivalent, or at least similar, to that of the 'Ruler of the synagogue' (Mark 5:22,35,36,38; Luke 8:49, 13:14), one appointed to supervise the external order in communal worship (Schurer, 2014). The welcome may have been similar to the following:

> Welcome, brothers and sisters, to this celebration of Breaking of Bread given us by Jesus! Just before His crucifixion, Jesus celebrated the Last Supper with His disciples, giving instructions that from then on we were to take bread and wine in memory of Him. At the Cross, Jesus our Messiah, the Son of God, took all our sin upon Himself, making a way for us to be reconciled to God and live in loving relationship with Him forever, walking and talking with Him each day. Sin separated us from God, but He loved us so much that He sent His Son to die in our place, bearing our sin and paying the penalty we deserved, so that we might be forgiven and become His sons and daughters.

The welcome is addressed to 'brothers and sisters' which was the customary greeting of the first century believers (Chadwick, 1967, p.32).

> *If there are unbelievers present:*
>
> If you have accepted Jesus as your Saviour, you are welcome to share in the bread and wine here today, but if you have not yet accepted Him, and you would like to, please raise your hand now and we will pray together, and in believing you will be saved. Repeat these words after me. We will all pray the prayer together:

Heavenly Father, / I know I am a sinner, / and I'm sorry for my sins. / I ask that You forgive me, / wash me and cleanse me, / from all unrighteousness. / I believe that Jesus / died for my sins / and rose from the dead. / Jesus said / that whoever / believes in Him / should not perish / but have / everlasting life. / So I believe in my heart / that Jesus died for my sins / and I believe / that God raised Him / from the dead / and He is alive. / I accept / Jesus Christ, / the risen Saviour / as my Lord / and my master. / I will do my best / to live for Him / to serve Him / and to walk together with Him / all the days of my life. / And according to His promise, / I'm washed, / I'm cleansed, / I'm justified, / I am saved.

Welcome to the Kingdom of God and to this Fellowship!

You will notice that this introduction contains an opportunity for any visiting non-believers to come to faith. Centuries later, the Eucharistic service would be divided into two sections, the first part being suitable for catechumens, those who were not yet baptised, and the second part being for baptised believers. But at this early point no such division existed. Therefore, it would have been necessary for whoever was leading to explain to visitors that only believers could take the bread and the wine, and give an opportunity for unbelievers to receive the Lord.

Announcements and notices are given.

The organisation and communication of the first church, implicit in Acts, likely found expression in communal meetings, where information and news of events were shared. We have therefore allowed for the inclusion of such announcements, placing these at the close of the fellowship meal so as not to draw attention away from the main focus of the service, which is the atoning sacrifice of Christ. This is the likely place in the first century Breaking of Bread service at which they would have welcomed everyone and shared announcements concerning events and information relating to the life of the church. At this point people would have finished their meals, making this a natural place for such notices.

The leader gives a call to worship (Heb. 'Barekhu'):

The meal and the announcements being concluded, the traditional Hebrew call to worship could then be given. This call, which commenced the synagogue services, is explicitly mentioned in the Mishnah, the earliest Jewish record of ordinances (Schurer, 2014). Being so familiar with it in the context of synagogue worship, it is likely that they commenced the new Breaking of Bread service in a similar way.

Leader:	LET US PRAISE. PRAISE THE LORD, WHO IS TO BE PRAISED!
All:	PRAISED IS THE LORD, WHO IS TO BE PRAISED FOR EVER AND EVER!
Leader:	PRAISED IS THE LORD, WHO IS TO BE PRAISED FOR EVER AND EVER!

Most likely, the leader would then open the service with an expression of praise to God. Such expressions, called *Berakah* (plural *Berakot*) in Hebrew were a familiar part of worship at that time. Recitation of the *Shema* (the reading of Deuteronomy 6:4-9, 11:13-21 and Numbers 15:37-41) in the first-century synagogue service on the Sabbath was preceded by one or two benedictions of this kind (Schurer, 2014), and this custom of opening with a blessing would likely have carried over to the new celebration of Breaking of Bread. Given that the Mishnah quotes the verse, 'Blessed be His glorious kingdom forever and ever' in conjunction with the *Shema* (Tamid 1:5, c.f. Psalm 72:19), we have chosen this blessing from Psalm 72:18,19 as perhaps the most likely candidate for inclusion here. We have also included the blessings of 1 Chronicles 16:36, 2 Chronicles 2:12, 2 Samuel 22:47, Nehemiah 9:5, Psalm 28:6, 68:19, 113:2, Ezekiel 3:12, and Daniel 2:20, as alternative or additional blessings.

One or more of the following blessings (Heb. 'Berakot') may be said:

Leader: THE LORD LIVES! AND BLESSED BE MY ROCK, AND EXALTED BE THE GOD OF THE ROCK OF MY SALVATION!

2 Samuel 22:47

All: AMEN!

Leader: BLESSED BE THE LORD GOD, THE GOD OF ISRAEL, WHO ONLY DOES WONDROUS THINGS! AND BLESSED BE HIS GLORIOUS NAME FOREVER! AND LET THE WHOLE EARTH BE FILLED WITH HIS GLORY.

Psalm 72:18,19

All: AMEN AND AMEN!

Leader: BLESSED BE THE LORD GOD OF ISRAEL FROM EVERLASTING TO EVERLASTING!

1 Chronicles 16:36

All: AMEN!

Leader: BLESSED BE THE LORD GOD OF ISRAEL, WHO MADE HEAVEN AND EARTH.

2 Chronicles 2:12

All: AMEN!

Leader: BLESSED BE YOUR GLORIOUS NAME, WHICH IS EXALTED ABOVE ALL BLESSING AND PRAISE!

Nehemiah 9:5

All: AMEN!

Leader: BLESSED BE THE LORD, BECAUSE HE HAS HEARD THE VOICE OF MY SUPPLICATIONS!

Psalm 28:6

All: AMEN!

Leader: BLESSED BE THE LORD, WHO DAILY LOADS US WITH BENEFITS, THE GOD OF OUR SALVATION!

Psalm 68:19

All: AMEN!

Leader: BLESSED IS THE NAME OF THE LORD, NOW AND FOREVER.

Psalm 113:2

All: AMEN!

Leader: BLESSED IS THE GLORY OF THE LORD FROM HIS PLACE!

Ezekiel 3:12

All: AMEN!

Leader: BLESSED BE THE NAME OF GOD FOREVER AND EVER, FOR WISDOM AND MIGHT ARE HIS.

Daniel 2:20

All: AMEN!

An opening hymn or psalm of praise may be sung.

At this point it is possible that they would have sung a hymn of praise. We know that they sang in worship in the first century, as the Jewish people had sung for centuries. We don't have any surviving scores from this period, but we do have the Book of Psalms, which has been called the hymn book of Israel. They would certainly have sung psalms.

(5) PRAYERS

Leader: Let us say together the prayer that Jesus taught us:

All: OUR FATHER,
WHO IS IN HEAVEN,
HALLOWED BE YOUR NAME,
YOUR KINGDOM COME,
YOUR WILL BE DONE,
ON EARTH, AS IT IS IN HEAVEN.
GIVE US THIS DAY OUR DAILY BREAD.
AND FORGIVE US OUR SINS,
AS WE FORGIVE THOSE WHO SIN AGAINST US.
AND LEAD US NOT INTO TEMPTATION,

BUT DELIVER US FROM THE EVIL ONE.
FOR YOURS IS THE KINGDOM,
THE POWER AND THE GLORY,
FOR EVER AND EVER.
AMEN.

From Matthew 6:9-13, Luke 11:2-4

The first Christian church had a rich treasury of material to draw upon for their meetings together. This would have included their experience of the Temple worship, their knowledge of the synagogue service every Sabbath, and also all that they had experienced through the wonderful ministry of the Lord Jesus Christ. Amongst the many things He taught them, there was one prayer in particular which would have been a part of their worship. This is the prayer we know as The Lord's Prayer. The earliest written mention of the Lord's Prayer in a Eucharistic context is made by Cyril of Jerusalem in 4 A.D. (Piédagnel, 1966), but given the significance of this prayer it is reasonable to assume that it was included from the beginning. It is inconceivable that the services of the first church would not at some point have included the prayer taught by Christ Himself (Matthew 6:9-13; Luke 11:2-4).

A prayer for the salvation of all may be said, either extemporaneously, or using the following example.

Leader: REMEMBER IN YOUR MERCY, O GOD OUR SAVIOUR, ALL KINGS AND ALL THAT ARE IN AUTHORITY, THAT WE MAY LEAD A QUIET AND PEACEABLE LIFE IN ALL GODLINESS AND REVERENCE, FOR THIS IS GOOD AND ACCEPTABLE IN YOUR SIGHT.

All: BLESSED ARE YOU, LORD, WHO MAKES PEACE.

Leader: REMEMBER IN YOUR MERCY, O GOD OUR SAVIOUR, ALL THOSE WHOM YOU HAVE CREATED, WHETHER ALIVE IN THE BODY, OR DEPARTED THIS LIFE. WE PRAY FOR ALL, THAT YOU WILL HAVE MERCY UPON EACH ONE, YOU

WHO DESIRE ALL TO BE SAVED AND TO COME TO THE KNOWLEDGE OF THE TRUTH. FOR THERE IS ONE GOD, AND ONE MEDIATOR BETWEEN GOD AND MEN, THE MAN CHRIST JESUS WHO GAVE HIMSELF A RANSOM FOR US ALL.

All: BLESSED ARE YOU, LORD, WHO MAKES THE DEAD ALIVE.

Leader: REMEMBER IN YOUR MERCY, O GOD OUR SAVIOUR, WE WHO CALL TO YOU NOW, THAT YOU WOULD VISIT US AND THOSE KNOWN TO US WHO ARE SUFFERING AT THIS TIME, THAT THROUGH THE MERITS OF YOUR CROSS WE MIGHT RECEIVE HEALING FROM SICKNESS, DELIVERANCE FROM AFFLICTION, AND GRACE TO HELP IN TIME OF NEED.

All: BLESSED ARE YOU, LORD, WHO HEARS PRAYER.

We can be sure that prayer for others was part of worship from the beginning, but it is not clear when the practice of praying for all began. Paul encourages it strongly in his letter to Timothy (1 Timothy 2:1-7) and the oldest prayer we have, outside of scripture, is a 'prayer for all needs' written by Clement, Bishop of Rome, in A.D.96 (Hamman, 1961). As the date of Clement's prayer lies outside our period, we have chosen instead to include a prayer for all based upon Paul's directions.

Included here is a prayer for all those departed this life. It is our view that, following the statement of Christ that the gates of Hades would not prevail against His church (Matthew 16:18), the first church prayed regularly for the unsaved dead that they might be reconciled to God through the Cross of Christ. The Breaking of Bread celebration, proclaiming Christ's victory over sin and death, would have been a natural context for such prayer.

(6) THE OFFERING FOR THE POOR

People come forward to the front and place their offering in the box or bag provided.

It would have been natural at this point, when everyone was thinking about the needs of others, for the first Christians to take up their offering. There was no pressure to give in the first church, but people being moved by love and compassion wanted to give what they could for the support of the poor and the relief of suffering amongst them. The first church had no paid ministers, so most, if not all, of what was given went to support outreach and those in need. It was only as the first century progressed that some church leaders began to be paid for their work out of church funds. The apostle Paul is notable in that, whilst acknowledging the right of leaders to be paid in this way, he refused to receive a salary from the church. He and the first apostles thus embodied the most noble position, labouring to provide for their own needs so that the church would not be burdened, thus ensuring the greatest funding for outreach and the relief of suffering.

At this point in the service people would come forward to the front where one or more of the apostles were sitting, and place their offering in the box or bag provided. All monies collected were put in a fund for the poorest members and distributed between them without partiality and according to need by the leaders of the congregation at another time.

It is written of the first church that, 'There was no one among them that lacked: for as many as were possessors of lands or houses sold them, and brought the prices of the things that were sold, and laid them at the apostles' feet: and distribution was made to every man according as he had need' (Acts 4:34,35). Commenting on this text, John Wesley says, 'It [money] is an excellent gift of God, answering the noblest ends. In the hands of His children, it is food for the hungry, drink for the thirsty, raiment for the naked: it gives to the traveller and the stranger where to lay his head. By it we may supply the place of a husband to the widow, and of a father to the fatherless. We may be a defence for the oppressed, a means of health to the sick, of ease to them that are in pain; it may be as eyes to the blind, as feet to the lame; yea, a lifter up from the gates of death' (Wesley, 1760).

This offering for the poor was made during the service (Romans 15:26; 2 Corinthians 9:13), and probably early in the service in the spirit of Psalm 96:8. We therefore place it here.

(7) STATEMENT OF FAITH

Leader: Let us boldly proclaim our faith:

All: CHRIST DIED FOR OUR SINS
IN ACCORDANCE WITH THE SCRIPTURES,
HE WAS BURIED,
AND HE WAS RAISED ON THE THIRD DAY
IN ACCORDANCE WITH THE SCRIPTURES.
HALLELUIA!

From 1 Corinthians 15:3,4

The proclamation of faith has been part of the life and worship of the church from the beginning. They did not have the creeds that are familiar to us, for these were developed centuries later, but they did have a creed, which is found in 1 Corinthians 15:3,4 and believed to date back to A.D. 30-35. This confession perfectly expresses the heart of our faith and is the earliest statement of belief known to us.

(8) PSALMS, HYMNS AND SPIRITUAL SONGS

One or more psalms, hymns or choruses may be sung.

By the time of Christ, worship in music and song had long been a part of the Jewish faith, and there is no reason to assume that this changed with the inception of the church. In fact, first century New

Testament texts assert that the singing of hymns, psalms and spiritual songs was a common and regular feature of both their worship together (1 Corinthians 14:26, Ephesians 5:18-19, Colossians 3:16, James 5:13) and their personal devotion (Acts 16:25). This was a community that sang (Cullmann, 1953), sometimes no doubt with musical instruments. In fact, the last hymn in their songbook, Psalm 150, encourages us to praise the LORD with every instrument and with every breath. First century instruments would have included the trumpet, the lute, the harp, the timbrel, stringed instruments, flutes, and cymbals. No doubt many of the hymns of first-century Judaism found their way into the sung worship of the infant church. Much of this material has been lost, but surviving documents have been catalogued (Charlesworth, 1986).

(9) SINGING IN TONGUES

Leader: Let us lift up our hearts and voices to God, singing in the Spirit.

Those gathered unite in praise and worship to God, singing in the Spirit.

For the first believers, worship in song would have easily led into singing in the spirit. This would have been a natural moment in the service for worshippers to start singing in tongues. The first church received the outpouring of the Holy Spirit on the Day of Pentecost, and speaking in tongues not known by the speaker was the first manifestation. From Pentecost on they enjoyed the operation of spiritual gifts, the Holy Spirit being freely given to all believers, fulfilling the promise of Jesus that 'The hour is coming, and now is, when the true worshippers will worship the Father in spirit and truth; for the Father is seeking such to worship Him. God is Spirit, and those who worship Him must worship in spirit and truth' (John 4:23,24). This Divine imperative was honoured by the church who sang with the angels in heavenly worship.

(10) HOLY SILENCE AND LISTENING TO GOD

Leader: Let us be still and silent in our hearts, listening to whatever God would say to us personally.

A minute's silence is held, listening to God in stillness and silence.

When the song of the Spirit ends, there is often a profound and living silence, for we have as it were, entered within the veil, and now stand in the Holy Place, the Throne Room of God. It is fitting that having come to this place, every tongue falls silent, and we listen to hear what He would say to us.

Deeply rooted in Old Testament history, the practice of stillness in prayer was affirmed by Jesus (see Luke 10:38-42), and maintained in the first church, both as a daily personal discipline and a collective act. It is suggested that this silence be kept for at least a minute in order to allow sufficient time for contemplation and reflection. Longer times of holy silence may be observed at vigils and special meetings, as well as in personal devotions.

In the words of Isaac the Syrian, 'He who desires to see the Lord within himself endeavours to purify his heart by the unceasing remembrance of God. The spiritual land of a man pure in soul is within him. The sun which shines in it is the light of the Holy Trinity. The air which its inhabitant breathes is the All-Holy Spirit. The life, joy and gladness of that country is Christ, the Light of the Light – the Father. That is the Jerusalem or Kingdom of God hidden within us, according to the word of the Lord. Try to enter the cell within you, and you will see the heavenly cell. They are one and the same. By one entry you enter both. The ladder to the Heavenly Kingdom is within you. It is built mysteriously in your soul' (Happold, 1970).

(11) REVELATION BY THE HOLY SPIRIT

Leader: Let us hear whatever the Lord would reveal to us, whether through words of wisdom or knowledge, through tongues with interpretation, or through prophecy.

Believers share what they have received from the Lord.

It was the practice of the first church for believers to make a contribution to the service, if they were inspired and moved by the Holy Spirit to do so. Hence Paul says: 'When you come together, each one has a hymn, a lesson, a revelation, a tongue, or an interpretation. Let all things be done for building up' (I Corinthians 14:26).

(12) THE CRY OF THE SERAPHIM

All: HOLY, HOLY, HOLY IS THE LORD OF HOSTS;
THE WHOLE EARTH IS FULL OF HIS GLORY!

Isaiah 6:3

Having drawn near to God, what could be more appropriate than to say or sing the 'thrice-holy hymn', the earliest form of which is found in the book of the prophet Isaiah (Isaiah 6:3), and would have been familiar to the Jewish worshippers of the first century.

A song or hymn of God's holiness may be sung.

(13) THE READING FROM THE HOLY GOSPEL

(STORIES OF CHRIST'S MINISTRY)

Reader: A READING FROM THE GOSPEL OF (BOOK), CHAPTER (N.), STARTING AT VERSE (N.)

The reader reads the Gospel text for the day, as given in the calendar of daily scripture readings throughout the year (Appendix A). Any member of the congregation may read. There may be one or more readers, who are invited to read by the leader.

We are used to some things today that did not exist at the inception of the first church at Jerusalem, and this includes the four written gospel accounts at the start of our New Testament. Whilst some scholars prefer later dates for the writing of the gospels, placing Mark from A.D.66-70, Matthew and Luke from A.D.85-90, and John from A.D.90-110, others believe that they may have been written much earlier, Matthew, Mark, and Luke as early as A.D.55, and John as early as A.D.80. Whether we support an earlier or a later date for their authorship, we must acknowledge that they were not there at the beginning. No one had a New Testament, because it had not yet been written. But they had something we do not have today. They had the apostles with them, and not just the apostles, there were multitudes of people who could tell their stories about Jesus (Mark 4:25; 5:1; Matthew 8:1,18; 9:8,33,36; 11:7; 12:15; 13:2; 14:22,23; 15:30; 19:2; 21:9; 26:55; Luke 5:15; 14:25; John 2:23; 4:39,41; 7:31,40; 8:30; 10:41,42; 11:45; 12:11,42).

When they came together people would have told these stories, encouraging and building up the church. If the earlier dates for the gospels are correct, the first church at Jerusalem would have had the synoptic gospels (Matthew, Mark and Luke) before the fall of Jerusalem in A.D.70, but until then, they relied upon what we call the oral tradition. The stories of Jesus were told by word of mouth. And this is a great proof of the authenticity of the gospel accounts which came to be written, because there were so very many witnesses! As H.E.W Turner points out, the fact that numerous eye witnesses were still alive at the time when the gospels were written ensures the veracity of what they wrote (Turner, 1963). We can trust the gospels. The events they describe, including the crucifixion, were so public and of such impact that news of them rapidly spread everywhere, becoming known by the leading historians of the age. Tacitus, historian of Imperial Rome, and no friend of Christianity, refers to the execution of Christ (Annals, 15.44), and the Jewish chronicler Josephus, refers to Jesus' 'marvellous deeds' (Antiquities, 18.3.3).

Gospel readings for every week of the year can be found in Appendix A.

(14) THE APOSTLES' TEACHING

Reader: A READING FROM (BOOK), CHAPTER (N.), STARTING AT VERSE (N.)

The reader reads the additional New Testament reading for the day, as given in the calendar of daily scripture readings throughout the year (Appendix A). Any member of the congregation may read. There may be one or more readers, who are invited to read by the leader.

Just as the four gospels were not yet written when the Jerusalem church began, so also the remainder of our New Testament had yet to be penned, but again, the apostles were there, bringing their teaching in person. For most of its short history, James, the Lord's brother was the leader of the Jerusalem church, and it is thought by some that his letter was written as early as A.D.45.

Today we have a New Testament full of inspired writings, mostly from the second half of the first century. We cannot listen to the apostles as they did, but we can hear their messages ringing out through the centuries from the wonderful texts that they wrote.

New Testament readings for every week of the year can be found in Appendix A.

(15) ONE OR MORE MESSAGES

Any members of the church who are moved by the Lord to share a brief word of encouragement or insight may now do so. These should be short and the speakers no more than three in number. The main speaker then brings the message he or she has prepared and concludes by praying for those gathered.

Luke asserts that the first church 'continued steadfastly in the apostles' teaching' (Acts 2:42) and the presence of preaching in worship is evidenced by Acts 20:7. Teaching would have been provided by those equipped to speak, and, as in the synagogue, could be given by any competent member of the congregation, with permission. It is recorded that both Jesus and Paul contributed to synagogue services in this way. One or more messages might be given. Just as in the synagogue of that day, it was the practice for a number of people to get up and share an insight or a message. Obviously, there would have been a limit on this, with most people sharing fairly briefly. The main speaker would take a little longer.

Preaching was centred on Christ: His life, person, cross, and resurrection. 'Unlike modern preaching which is usually either the logical development of some topic or the elaboration of a single text, the apostolic preaching was a narration of the life and work of Jesus, with a defence of His resurrection, and was followed by a call to repentance and faith in His name' (Tenney, 1961). As J.G. Lake says, 'No other service in the world gives us better or equal opportunity to express the wonderful truth of redemption' (Lake, 1921). The message of the Cross was central.

The style of preaching and teaching would have been interactive. Just as Jesus had encouraged open discussion and dialogue with His hearers, so the apostles would also have actively engaged in discussion and discourse.

(16) REPENTANCE

Leader: Let us examine our hearts and our lives, confessing our sins to Almighty God in silent prayer, and turning from them in repentance and faith.

A moment of silent reflection and repentance.

The significance of repentance for Jewish believers has already been noted. They did not consider that the Cross made further repentance unnecessary for the believer, but held to the view, later expressed in the first epistle of John, that their fellowship with God required a life of ongoing repentance from sin (1 John 1:5-10).

(17) PRAYERS OF HEALING & CONSECRATION

There may be prayers for specific needs, including prayer for healing and deliverance. Here there may also be the consecration of individuals to tasks, missions, roles and ministries.

It is clear from the gospels and Acts that prayer for those in need was central to the ministry of both Christ and the apostles, and would thus have had its place in the meetings of the church. Just as in the church today, sometimes there would have been specific matters needing prayer, such as prayer for healing if there were sick people amongst them, or prayers of consecration if there was a need to appoint people to specific roles in the fellowship.

(18) THANKSGIVING

Leader: Let us give thanks to God for the sacrifice of the Cross and the new life we have thereby received.

Believers take turns in giving thanks to God for the Cross.

It is likely that from its inception the first church would have given thanks for the sacrifice of Christ and for the eternal benefits He won through the Cross for all those who believe. Such thanksgiving would have been extemporaneous.

A song or hymn on the message of the Cross or on the blood of Jesus may be sung.

We cannot be sure, but it is not unlikely that, at least sometimes, a song or hymn would be sung at this point celebrating the triumph of the Cross!

(19) THE BREAKING OF BREAD

The leader reads the words of institution spoken by Our Lord and Saviour at the Last Supper on the night in which He was betrayed.

Leader: THE LORD JESUS ON THE SAME NIGHT IN WHICH HE WAS BETRAYED TOOK BREAD; AND WHEN HE HAD GIVEN THANKS, HE BROKE IT AND SAID, 'TAKE, EAT; THIS IS MY BODY WHICH IS BROKEN FOR YOU; DO THIS IN REMEMBRANCE OF ME.'

IN THE SAME MANNER HE ALSO TOOK THE CUP AFTER SUPPER, SAYING, 'THIS CUP IS THE NEW COVENANT IN MY BLOOD. THIS DO, AS OFTEN AS YOU DRINK IT, IN REMEMBRANCE OF ME.'

The bread and wine are then distributed to all, the bread having been broken into pieces beforehand, and individual glasses or cups having been made ready.

The leader invites all those that are born again to take the bread, repeating Christ's words, 'Take eat; this is My body which is broken for you; do this in remembrance of Me.'

The leader invites all those that are born again to take the wine, repeating Christ's words, 'This cup is the cup of the New Covenant in My blood. This do, as often as you drink it, in remembrance of Me.'

Having received the bread and wine, those present open their hearts to God, asking Him to fill them afresh with His Holy Spirit.

Now we come to the greatest part of our service, the breaking of bread in memory of Christ's sacrifice of Himself for us. Luke tells us that the first church 'continued steadfastly in ... the breaking of bread' (Acts 2:42). This act was at the heart of their life together.

At this point the leader would remind everyone present of Jesus words at the Last Supper when He established the practice of taking bread and wine in this way. Having been present with Christ at the last supper, the apostles would have recalled His words of institution and repeated them at the Breaking of Bread. The apostle Paul, though not present at the last supper was familiar with Jesus' words, and narrates them in 1 Corinthians 11:23-26, from which our text is taken.

The bread and the wine would then be distributed, before all were invited to take first the bread and then the wine. The leader would likely repeat Christ's words of institution at this point.

Having received the bread and wine, those present open their hearts to God, asking Him to fill them afresh with His Holy Spirit.

The first believers knew the need to be anointed [Heb. 'overflowed'] with fresh oil [a Biblical symbol of the Holy Spirit]

(Psalm 92:10). Their experience of the Spirit's outpouring at Pentecost was the foundation for a new and hitherto unknown level of Divine empowerment. From that Pentecost on, the receipt of the Holy Spirit was normative for believers so that anyone who desired to be filled and led by the Spirit would only have to ask God and they would receive. In pouring out His Spirit upon all, God demonstrated His desire for each and every one of us to be supremely and supernaturally empowered in this way. The last words of Christ to His disciples before He ascended were to wait in Jerusalem until they were filled with the Holy Spirit, the promise of the Father. This was a command to all believers in every generation, for without the Holy Spirit we can accomplish nothing of eternal value. It is folly and presumption to try and do anything until we are baptised with the Spirit!

(20) THE BLESSING

When all those present have shared in Christ's body and blood, the leader gives the blessing:

Leader: THE LORD BLESS YOU, AND KEEP YOU.
THE LORD MAKE HIS FACE SHINE UPON YOU,
AND BE GRACIOUS TO YOU.
THE LORD LIFT UP HIS COUNTENANCE UPON YOU,
AND GIVE YOU PEACE.

Numbers 6:24-26

All: AMEN.

When everyone has taken the bread and the wine, the service ends with the blessing that God's people had used for centuries. This blessing was given by God Himself. He spoke to Moses, and said, 'Speak to Aaron and his sons, saying, "This is the way you shall bless the children of Israel."' It is recorded in the Bible, in the book of Numbers, chapter 6, verses 22 to 26. As in the Temple services and the synagogue liturgy of the first century, it is to be expected that the Breaking of Bread service would have concluded with this Aaronic blessing.

In time, additional blessings would be written, including that of 1 Thessalonians 5:23,24,28, which may be used as an alternative. Paul's first letter to the church at Thessalonica, believed to have been written at Corinth in A.D. 50-51, may be one of the earliest New Testament books to be written. It is therefore possible that this blessing, or one like it, was also used by the first century Jerusalem church in its last two decades, or even before. The words 'The grace of our Lord Jesus Christ be with you,' may have themselves been taken from the weekly liturgical use of the church.

(21) CLOSING HYMN

A concluding hymn may be sung.

We cannot be certain whether the first believers concluded their breaking of bread service with a hymn, but we do know that Jesus ended the Last Supper in this way. Thus it is not unlikely that the early believers followed His example. We do not know what they sang. It was no doubt a song of praise familiar to them all, perhaps even the 'hymn to Christ as God' referred to by Pliny the Younger in his letter to Trajan around A.D.112.

AFTER THE SERVICE

After the service, pieces of the blessed bread are taken to the sick, those in prison, and any others who were prevented from attending the service.

It is likely that after the service, pieces of the blessed bread were taken to the sick and those in prison. As Chadwick points out, 'To share in this sacred meal [the 'breaking of bread'] was so deeply felt to be the essential expression of membership of the society that fragments of the broken bread were taken round to any who were absent through illness or imprisonment' (Chadwick, 1967, p.32).

USING THIS SERVICE TODAY

Jesus Christ is the same yesterday, today, and forever.

Hebrews 13:8

We hope that through the publication of this reconstructed first-century Eucharist, believers today will be encouraged to celebrate the Breaking of Bread in their homes, as Christ's followers did at the beginning. As we have seen, the Breaking of Bread would have originally taken place in homes on a Saturday evening, but there is no reason why it should not also be celebrated at other times. Similarly, there is no reason why it should not be celebrated in any appropriate location, including buildings designated for church use.

Given that we cannot be certain regarding the order of the components in the Breaking of Bread service, we may be encouraged to vary that order as we feel it appropriate. If you are holding your own Breaking of Bread service, as we hope you will, you may wish to change the order, as you are led by the Holy Spirit. We do not believe that there was a fixed outline followed in exactly the same way on every occasion, but that there was flexibility and variety in the life and worship of the first Christian community.

(1) PREPARATION

Those attending prepare their hearts through remembrance of the Cross, repentance and forgiveness, to share in the body and blood of Christ.

The place is prepared, with bread and wine ready.

Personal preparation is as important today as it ever was. We ought to examine our hearts before the Lord, repenting of our sin and re-consecrating our life to Him.

If food is prepared at the venue, strict standards of culinary hygiene should be observed. The bread and red wine used in the service may be of any kind. We advise that the wine is served in individual glasses so as to avoid the risk of infection from contagious diseases, and that the bread is broken into small individual portions prior to the service. Strict standards of hygiene should be followed, both in the preparation of the fellowship meal and the preparation of the bread and wine.

(2) ARRIVALS AND GREETINGS

As people arrive they greet one another, sharing the peace of God.

Wherever conditions are suitable the Kiss of Peace is a fine greeting. However, the 'holy kiss' may not always be the most appropriate form of the greeting. We advise that personal, cultural, health and safeguarding considerations are all taken into account in choosing how we greet one another. It is not the form of the greeting but the heart and intention of the saint that matters. If the heart is right with God, the mere presence of the believer brings peace. In fact, in the eastern church one of the finest things that may be said of someone is that their presence is a benediction of peace.

Thus we uphold the ancient practise of sharing God's peace with others, but with discretion as to how we share. Where the kiss of peace is given, we suggest that, following first century practice, it is only exchanged between members of the same gender.

(3) THE FELLOWSHIP MEAL

People take their places for the fellowship meal, and a member of the community gives thanks to God.

The fellowship meal can be as simple or as elaborate as desired. It may be prepared at the home, or it may be delivered by a local restaurant. In order to protect the vulnerable, we advise that there are no alcoholic drinks at the fellowship meal. Given both human weakness and the wiles of Satan, this is an important safeguard which should not be disregarded in our view, particularly in public gatherings.

(4) WELCOME AND ANNOUNCEMENTS

After the meal everyone is welcomed and necessary announcements of information and events in the life of the church are made. The leader, host, or another representative of the community, introduces the service, either in their own words, or using a welcome such as the following:

Welcome, brothers and sisters, to this celebration of Breaking of Bread given us by Jesus! Just before His crucifixion, Jesus celebrated the Last Supper with His disciples, giving instructions that from then on we were to take bread and wine in memory of Him. At the Cross, Jesus our Messiah, the Son of God, took all our sin upon Himself, making a way for us to be reconciled to God and live in loving relationship with Him forever, walking and talking with Him each day. Sin separated us from God, but He loved us so much that He sent His Son to die in our place, bearing our sin and paying the penalty we deserved, so that we might be forgiven and become His sons and daughters.

If there are unbelievers present:

If you have accepted Jesus as your Saviour, you are welcome to share in the bread and wine here today, but if you have not yet accepted Him, and you would like to, please raise your hand now and we will pray together, and in believing you will be saved. Repeat these words after me. We will all pray the prayer together:

Heavenly Father, / I know I am a sinner, / and I'm sorry for my sins. / I ask that You forgive me, / wash me and cleanse me, / from all unrighteousness. / I believe that Jesus / died for my sins / and rose from the dead. / Jesus said / that whoever / believes in Him / should not perish / but have / everlasting life. / So I believe in my heart / that Jesus died for my sins / and I believe / that God raised Him / from the dead / and He is alive. / I accept / Jesus Christ, / the risen Saviour / as my Lord / and my master. / I will do my best / to live for Him / to serve Him / and to walk together with Him / all the days of my life. / And according to His promise, / I am washed, / I am cleansed, / I am justified, / I am saved.

Welcome to the Kingdom of God and to this Fellowship!

Where non-believers are present and an invitation to faith is given, it is suggested that the whole group prays the prayer of commitment together, making it easier for the respondent. At the conclusion of the service those who have made a commitment are welcomed, their details taken, and arrangements made to meet with them.

Announcements and notices are given.

The leader gives a call to worship (Heb. 'Barekhu'):

Leader: LET US PRAISE.
PRAISE THE LORD, WHO IS TO BE PRAISED!

All: PRAISED IS THE LORD, WHO IS TO BE PRAISED FOR EVER AND EVER!

Leader: PRAISED IS THE LORD, WHO IS TO BE PRAISED FOR EVER AND EVER

One or more of the following blessings (Heb. 'Berakot') may be said:

Leader: THE LORD LIVES! AND BLESSED BE MY ROCK, AND EXALTED BE THE GOD OF THE ROCK OF MY SALVATION!

2 Samuel 22:47

All: AMEN!

Leader: BLESSED BE THE LORD GOD, THE GOD OF ISRAEL, WHO ONLY DOES WONDROUS THINGS! AND BLESSED BE HIS GLORIOUS NAME FOREVER! AND LET THE WHOLE EARTH BE FILLED WITH HIS GLORY.

Psalm 72:18,19

All: AMEN AND AMEN!

Leader: BLESSED BE THE LORD GOD OF ISRAEL FROM EVERLASTING TO EVERLASTING!

1 Chronicles 16:36

All: AMEN!

Leader: BLESSED BE THE LORD GOD OF ISRAEL, WHO MADE HEAVEN AND EARTH.

2 Chronicles 2:12

All: AMEN!

Leader: BLESSED BE YOUR GLORIOUS NAME, WHICH IS EXALTED ABOVE ALL BLESSING AND PRAISE!

Nehemiah 9:5

All: AMEN!

Leader: BLESSED BE THE LORD, BECAUSE HE HAS HEARD THE VOICE OF MY SUPPLICATIONS!

Psalm 28:6

All: AMEN!

Leader: BLESSED BE THE LORD, WHO DAILY LOADS US WITH BENEFITS, THE GOD OF OUR SALVATION!

Psalm 68:19

All: AMEN!

Leader: BLESSED IS THE NAME OF THE LORD, NOW AND FOREVER. Psalm 113:2

All: AMEN!

Leader: BLESSED IS THE GLORY OF THE LORD FROM HIS PLACE! Ezekiel 3:12

All: AMEN!

Leader: BLESSED BE THE NAME OF GOD FOREVER AND EVER, FOR WISDOM AND MIGHT ARE HIS. Daniel 2:20

All: AMEN!

In order to enable as many people as possible to actively participate in the service, all these blessings may be spoken, each one being proclaimed by a different person.

An opening hymn or psalm of praise may be sung.

(5) PRAYERS

Leader: Let us say together the prayer that Jesus taught us:

All: OUR FATHER,
WHO IS IN HEAVEN,
HALLOWED BE YOUR NAME,
YOUR KINGDOM COME,
YOUR WILL BE DONE,
ON EARTH, AS IT IS IN HEAVEN.
GIVE US THIS DAY OUR DAILY BREAD.
AND FORGIVE US OUR SINS,
AS WE FORGIVE THOSE WHO SIN AGAINST US.
AND LEAD US NOT INTO TEMPTATION,
BUT DELIVER US FROM THE EVIL ONE.
FOR YOURS IS THE KINGDOM,
THE POWER AND THE GLORY,
FOR EVER AND EVER. AMEN.

From Matthew 6:9-13, Luke 11:2-4

A prayer for the salvation of all may be said, either extemporaneously, or using the following example.

	REMEMBER IN YOUR MERCY, O GOD OUR SAVIOUR, ALL KINGS AND ALL THAT ARE IN AUTHORITY, THAT WE MAY LEAD A QUIET AND PEACEABLE LIFE IN ALL GODLINESS AND REVERENCE, FOR THIS IS GOOD AND ACCEPTABLE IN YOUR SIGHT.
All:	BLESSED ARE YOU, LORD, WHO MAKES PEACE.
Leader:	REMEMBER IN YOUR MERCY, O GOD OUR SAVIOUR, ALL THOSE WHOM YOU HAVE CREATED, WHETHER ALIVE IN THE BODY, OR DEPARTED THIS LIFE. WE PRAY FOR ALL, THAT YOU WILL HAVE MERCY UPON EACH ONE, YOU WHO DESIRE ALL TO BE SAVED AND TO COME TO THE KNOWLEDGE OF THE TRUTH. FOR THERE IS ONE GOD, AND ONE MEDIATOR BETWEEN GOD AND MEN, THE MAN CHRIST JESUS WHO GAVE HIMSELF A RANSOM FOR US ALL.
All:	BLESSED ARE YOU, LORD, WHO MAKES THE DEAD ALIVE.
Leader:	REMEMBER IN YOUR MERCY, O GOD OUR SAVIOUR, WE WHO CALL TO YOU NOW, THAT YOU WOULD VISIT US AND THOSE KNOWN TO US WHO ARE SUFFERING AT THIS TIME, THAT THROUGH THE MERITS OF YOUR CROSS WE MIGHT RECEIVE HEALING FROM SICKNESS, DELIVERANCE FROM AFFLICTION, AND GRACE TO HELP IN TIME OF NEED.
All:	BLESSED ARE YOU, LORD, WHO HEARS PRAYER.

Other prayers may be included here, as required. Incense may also be burnt if desired. Whilst many hold that the first Christians did not use incense in their worship (Bradshaw, 1992), this is by no means certain, particularly as the relation between prayer and incense was an established part of the Jewish culture: 'Let my prayer be set before You as incense, the lifting up of my hands as the evening sacrifice' (Psalm 141:2). Moreover, in his revelation, written towards the end of the first century, the apostle John underlines and affirms the role of incense in the worship of Heaven (Revelation 5:8; 8:3f.).

(6) THE OFFERING FOR THE POOR

People come forward to the front and place their offering in the box or bag provided.

In relation to giving and the administration of funds we advise that two people are involved in the counting and recording of the offering. Decisions regarding the giving of the church should be made by pastoral leaders who are properly informed regarding the needs of the flock in their area.

(7) STATEMENT OF FAITH

Leader: Let us boldly proclaim our faith:

All: CHRIST DIED FOR OUR SINS
IN ACCORDANCE WITH THE SCRIPTURES,
HE WAS BURIED,
AND HE WAS RAISED ON THE THIRD DAY
IN ACCORDANCE WITH THE SCRIPTURES.
HALLELUIA!

From 1 Corinthians 15:3,4

Impromptu and unscripted proclamations of faith may also be made.

(8) PSALMS, HYMNS AND SPIRITUAL SONGS

One or more psalms, hymns or choruses may be sung.

Given that early Christian worship in song included the singing of psalms, of hymns, and of spiritual songs, some of which would have been composed by members, it seems appropriate that any contemporary re-enactment allows for a similarly rich mix of items, drawing from the Psalms, the inspiration of members, and the great hymns and worship songs of every age.

(9) SINGING IN TONGUES

Leader: Let us lift up our hearts and voices to God, singing in the Spirit.

Those gathered unite in praise and worship to God, singing in the Spirit.

This is, of course, an expression of worship which we may use at any time, and not merely during times of group praise. A preacher once said that he liked to sing in tongues when he was buying his groceries. He would pass through the store singing in the Spirit. One day someone asked him, 'What are you doing?' to which he replied, 'I'm singing a song my father taught me.' That's just what this is. When we sing in the Spirit, we sing the songs of our Father in heaven.

(10) HOLY SILENCE AND LISTENING TO GOD

Leader: Let us be still and silent in our hearts, listening to whatever God would say to us personally.

A minute's silence is held, listening to God in stillness and silence.

To sit at the Lord's feet in loving adoration, listening attentively to Him, will always be the first and greatest joy of the Christian. As

Jesus said of Mary, 'One thing is needful' (Luke 10:42). It is reported of the great 18th century evangelist George Whitefield that having stayed at the home of a man given to materialism, he took a diamond and inscribed this phrase on the window of the room in which he had lodged. It remains there to this day, witness to these immortal words of Our Saviour (Dallimore, 1980).

Whatever we receive from God we ought to take to heart, for His words to us will be by far the most important words we hear in this life. Consider keeping a journal in which you record His word to you each day. Jesus said, 'My sheep hear My voice' (John 10:27), and this is important because there are many voices that speak in the human mind, including those of the demons, who will try to trick us. Don't allow this to stop you listening to God, but persevere in seeking Him, listening to Him each day, and in time your spiritual senses will become trained through practice to discern between good and evil (Hebrews 5:14).

(11) REVELATION BY THE HOLY SPIRIT

Leader: Let us hear whatever the Lord would reveal to us, whether through words of wisdom or knowledge, through tongues with interpretation, or through prophecy.

Believers share what they have received from the Lord.

The first church enjoyed a rich expression of spiritual gifts. These were to be exercised in an orderly way and for the benefit of all. The directions given by Paul, and recorded in 1 Corinthians 12-14, give us an excellent example of the kind of guidelines that would have been given by the apostolic leaders of the early Christian community. We do well to follow them, wherever the gifts of the Spirit are in operation.

(12) THE CRY OF THE SERAPHIM

All: HOLY, HOLY, HOLY IS THE LORD OF HOSTS;
THE WHOLE EARTH IS FULL OF HIS GLORY!

Isaiah 6:3

A song or hymn of God's holiness may be sung.

If desired, this proclamation may be followed by a hymn or other Bible texts expressing God's holiness (e.g., Revelation 4:8).

(13) THE READING FROM THE HOLY GOSPEL
(STORIES OF CHRIST'S MINISTRY)

Reader: A READING FROM THE GOSPEL OF (BOOK), CHAPTER (N.), STARTING AT VERSE (N.)

The reader reads the Gospel text for the day, as given in the calendar of daily scripture readings throughout the year (Appendix A). Any member of the congregation may read. There may be one or more readers, who are invited to read by the leader.

All believers should be encouraged to take a turn in reading at some point. Many of the Gospel readings in the calendar are two chapters long, enabling two readers to read a chapter each.

(14) THE APOSTLES' TEACHING

Reader: THE MESSAGE FROM THE HOLY APOSTLE (N.) IN (NAME OF BOOK), CHAPTER (N.), READING FROM VERSE (N.)

The reader reads the additional New Testament reading for the day, as given in the calendar of daily scripture readings throughout the year (Appendix A). Any member of the congregation may read. There may be one or more readers, who are invited to read by the leader.

Again, all should be encouraged to take turns in reading at services. Readings from the apostles' teaching are two or more chapters long, enabling a number of readers to take part.

(15) ONE OR MORE MESSAGES

Any members of the church who are moved by the Lord to share a brief word of encouragement or insight may now do so. These should be short and the speakers no more than three in number. The main speaker then brings the message he or she has prepared and concludes by praying for those gathered.

The leader invites those who have a brief word of encouragement to come forward and share it with the congregation. This is followed by the main message.

(16) PRAYERS OF HEALING & CONSECRATION

There may be prayers for specific needs, including prayer for healing and deliverance. Here there may also be the consecration of individuals to tasks, missions, roles and ministries.

People with needs may be invited forwards for prayer. Whilst some may have specific gifts of healings, it should be taught that all disciples of the Lord Jesus Christ may pray in faith for healing, both for themselves and others.

(17) REPENTANCE

Leader: Let us examine our hearts and our lives, confessing our sins to Almighty God in silent prayer, and turning from them in repentance and faith.

A moment of silent reflection and repentance.

The leader introduces a time of repentance. Following a short time of silence, he or she may pray a general prayer of repentance, if desired. In this respect we would recommend Psalm 51:1-17, which may be said or sung together. First century Jewish believers would have been familiar with this prayer of repentance spoken by King David when Nathan the prophet challenged him after he had gone in to Bathsheba.

(18) THANKSGIVING

Leader: Let us give thanks to God for the sacrifice of the Cross and the new life we have thereby received.

Believers take turns in giving thanks to God for the Cross.

A song or hymn on the message of the Cross or on the blood of Jesus may be sung.

At this point, immediately prior to the sharing of the bread and wine, it is most evidently fitting for a song or hymn to be sung celebrating the triumph of the Cross and the shed blood of Jesus!

(19) THE BREAKING OF BREAD

The leader reads the words of institution spoken by Our Lord and Saviour at the Last Supper on the night in which He was betrayed.

Leader: THE LORD JESUS ON THE SAME NIGHT IN WHICH HE WAS BETRAYED TOOK BREAD; AND WHEN HE HAD GIVEN THANKS, HE BROKE IT AND SAID, 'TAKE, EAT; THIS IS MY BODY WHICH IS BROKEN FOR YOU; DO THIS IN REMEMBRANCE OF ME.'

IN THE SAME MANNER HE ALSO TOOK THE CUP AFTER SUPPER, SAYING, 'THIS CUP IS THE NEW COVENANT IN

> MY BLOOD. THIS DO, AS OFTEN AS YOU DRINK IT, IN REMEMBRANCE OF ME.'

The bread and wine are then distributed to all, the bread having been broken into pieces beforehand, and individual glasses or cups having been made ready.

The leader invites all those that are born again to take the bread, repeating Christ's words, 'Take eat; this is My body which is broken for you; do this in remembrance of Me.'

The leader invites all those that are born again to take the wine, repeating Christ's words, 'This cup is the cup of the New Covenant in My blood. This do, as often as you drink it, in remembrance of Me.'

In order to safeguard health, we advise that instead of everyone drinking from one cup, the wine is poured into a number of individual cups or glasses, so that everyone has their own cup to drink from. Similarly, we advise that the bread be cut into pieces before the service.

The question often arises as to whether wine or grape juice should be used. We leave this to the discretion of those leading the service, believing that whichever is chosen it fully represents the blood of Christ.

Having received the bread and wine, those present open their hearts to God, asking Him to fill them afresh with His Holy Spirit.

Having received the bread and wine, we may ask our Father to fill us afresh with His Holy Spirit (Ephesians 5:18), and He will.

(20) THE BLESSING

When all those present have shared in Christ's body and blood, the leader gives the blessing:

Leader: THE LORD BLESS YOU, AND KEEP YOU.
THE LORD MAKE HIS FACE SHINE UPON YOU,
AND BE GRACIOUS TO YOU.
THE LORD LIFT UP HIS COUNTENANCE UPON YOU,
AND GIVE YOU PEACE.

Numbers 6:24-26

All: AMEN.

Alternatively, the blessing from 2 Corinthians 13:14 may be used:

THE GRACE OF THE LORD JESUS CHRIST, AND THE LOVE OF GOD, AND THE COMMUNION OF THE HOLY SPIRIT BE WITH YOU ALL. AMEN.

Or simply: THE GRACE OF OUR LORD JESUS CHRIST BE WITH YOU ALL. AMEN.

The basic formula here is found in Romans 16:20; 1 Corinthians 16:23; Galatians 6:18; Philippians 4:23; 1 Thessalonians 5:28; 2 Thessalonians 3:18; Titus 3:15; Philemon 25; and Hebrews 13:25.

(21) CLOSING HYMN

A concluding hymn may be sung.

Just as they likely sang a closing song or hymn at the first-century Breaking of Bread services, so may we. Any Christian hymn, psalm or worship song may be chosen.

AFTER THE SERVICE

After the service, pieces of the blessed bread are taken to the sick, those in prison, and any others who were prevented from attending the service.

APPENDIX A

USING THIS CALENDAR

The following chart gives suggested readings for both the first-century Sabbath Service and the Breaking of Bread Service. Whilst the Breaking of Bread was undoubtedly the central meeting of the first church, they would also in time have developed their own Sabbath Service and this probably took place early on the Sabbath, that is after sunset on Friday evening, which was the start of the Jewish day.

The first Christians observed the first day of the week rather than the seventh (John 20:1,19,26-29; Acts 20:6-12; 1 Corinthians 16:1-2). They were no longer under a legal requirement to keep the Sabbath, because all the Jewish Sabbaths with the Mosaic law were done away through the Cross of Christ and the establishment of a new and better covenant. The apostles did not require that the law and the Sabbath should be kept (Acts 15:5-29; Romans 14:5-6; Galatians 4:9-11; Colossians 2:14-17). But the law, being now engraved on the hearts of men, inspired them to live according to God, and this included the keeping of a day of rest, which might now be any day of the week.

The Jewish Sabbath service played a valuable role in biblical education and it is not surprising that the first church recognised this and therefore made it their own. This service included readings from the Law (the first five books of the Bible) and the Prophets, whilst the Breaking of Bread Service would have included stories of Jesus (the Gospels are our equivalent) and the teaching of the Apostles (equivalent to the remainder of our New Testament). Our chart reflects this historic distinction.

The Old Testament readings include all the books considered canonical by the ancient Christian community. These are the books found in the Greek version of the Old Testament known as the Septuagint (LXX). Some of these books may be unfamiliar to modern readers, as both the Roman Catholic and Protestant Old Testaments contain a reduced number of books. The Septuagint 'was the Christian Bible for both Greeks and Latins, the Bible of the apostles' (Chadwick, 2001). For a Bible that contains this complete Old Testament text, see 'The Orthodox Study Bible,' Thomas Nelson, 2008.

The readings for the Breaking of Bread Service enable the whole of the New Testament to be read in one year, whilst those for the Sabbath Service enable the whole of the Pentateuch to be read in one year. In this we follow the practice of the Babylonian Talmud in which the entire Pentateuch was read through in a year, interrupted only by special readings for the festivals (Bradshaw, 1992). The remainder of the Old Testament is read over a period of seven years.

This chart is also suitable for personal use, enabling the whole Bible to be read in one year. Readings are given for each week, and in the case of the additional Old Testament readings (the 'Prophets'), for each day.

The chart has deliberately been left undated by year so as to permit its use in any year.

READINGS FOR THE SABBATH AND BREAKING OF BREAD SERVICES

A CALENDAR OF DAILY SCRIPTURE READINGS THROUGHOUT THE YEAR

For use in the weekly services of the First Church of Jerusalem, as well as for personal reading and reflection, covering all the books of the Bible in one year, including the apocryphal Old Testament books

CALENDAR	Readings from the Pentateuch for The Sabbath Service	Additional Old Testament Readings for The Sabbath Service	Readings from the Gospels for The Breaking of Bread	Additional New Testament Readings for The Breaking of Bread
Week 1 **1 - 7 Jan** 1 Jan 2 Jan 3 Jan 4 Jan 5 Jan 6 Jan 7 Jan	**Genesis** **1:1-6:8**	**Joshua 1-17** Jos.1-3 Jos.4-5 Jos.6,7 Jos.8-10 Jos.11,12 Jos.13,14 Jos.15-17	**Matthew** **1,2**	**Acts** **1,2**
Week 2 **8 - 14 Jan** 8 Jan 9 Jan 10 Jan 11 Jan 12 Jan 13 Jan 14 Jan	**Genesis** **6:9-11:32**	**Joshua 18-24** **& Judges 1-9** Jos.18,19 Jos.20,21 Jos.22-24 Jdg.1,2 Jdg.3,4 Jdg.5-7 Jdg.8,9	**Matthew** **3,4**	**Acts** **3,4**

Week 3 15 - 21 Jan 15 Jan 16 Jan 17 Jan 18 Jan 19 Jan 20 Jan 21 Jan	Genesis 12:1-17:27	Judges 10-21 & Ruth Jdg.10,11 Jdg.12-14 Jdg.15,16 Jdg.17,18 Jdg.19-21 Ru.1,2 Ru.3,4	Matthew 5,6	Acts 5,6
Week 4 22 - 28 Jan 22 Jan 23 Jan 24 Jan 25 Jan 26 Jan 27 Jan 28 Jan	Genesis 18:1-22:24	1 Samuel 1-17 1 Sa.1-3 1 Sa.4,5 1 Sa.6,7 1 Sa.8-10 1 Sa.11,12 1 Sa.13,14 1 Sa.15-17	Matthew 7,8	Acts 7,8
Week 5 29 Jan - 4 Feb 29 Jan 30 Jan 31 Jan 1 Feb 2 Feb 3 Feb 4 Feb	Genesis 23:1-25:18	1 Samuel 18-31 & 2 Samuel 1-2 1 Sa.18,19 1 Sa.20,21 1 Sa.22-24 1 Sa.25,26 1 Sa.27,28 1 Sa.29-31 2 Sa.1,2	Matthew 9,10	Acts 9,10
Week 6 5 - 11 Feb 5 Feb 6 Feb 7 Feb 8 Feb 9 Feb 10 Feb 11 Feb	Genesis 25:19-28:9	2 Samuel 3-18 2 Sa.3,4 2 Sa.5-7 2 Sa.8,9 2 Sa.10,11 2 Sa.12-14 2 Sa.15,16 2 Sa.17,18	Matthew 11,12	Acts 11,12

Week 7 **12 - 18 Feb** 12 Feb 13 Feb 14 Feb 15 Feb 16 Feb 17 Feb 18 Feb	**Genesis** **28:10-32:3**	**2 Samuel 19-24 & 1 Kings 1-11** 2 Sa.19-21 2 Sa.22-24 1 Ki.1,2 1 Ki.3,4 1 Ki.5-7 1 Ki.8,9 1 Ki.10,11	**Matthew** **13,14**	**Acts** **13,14**
Week 8 **19 - 25 Feb** 19 Feb 20 Feb 21 Feb 22 Feb 23 Feb 24 Feb 25 Feb	**Genesis** **32:4-36:43**	**1 Kings 12-22** 1 Ki.12-14 1 Ki.15,16 1 Ki.17,18 1 Ki.19,20 1 Ki.21,22 2 Ki.1-3 2 Ki.4,5	**Matthew** **15,16**	**Acts** **15,16**
Week 9 **26 Feb - 4Mar** 26 Feb 27 Feb 28/29 Feb 1 Mar 2 Mar 3 Mar 4 Mar	**Genesis** **37:1-40:23**	**2 Kings 6-21** 2 Ki.6,7 2 Ki.8-10 2 Ki.11,12 2 Ki.13,14 2 Ki.15-17 2 Ki.18,19 2 Ki.20,21	**Matthew** **17,18**	**Acts** **17,18**
Week 10 **5 - 11 Mar** 5 Mar 6 Mar 7 Mar 8 Mar 9 Mar 10 Mar 11 Mar	**Genesis** **41:1-44:17**	**2 Kings 22-25 & 1 Chronicles 1-12** 2 Ki.22,23 2 Ki.24,25 1 Ch.1-3 1 Ch.4,5 1 Ch.6,7 1 Ch.8-10 1 Ch.11,12	**Matthew** **19,20**	**Acts** **19-21**

Week 11 **12 - 18 Mar** 12 Mar 13 Mar 14 Mar 15 Mar 16 Mar 17 Mar 18 Mar	**Genesis** **44:18-47:27**	**1 Chronicles** **13-29** 1 Ch.13,14 1 Ch.15-17 1 Ch.18,19 1 Ch.20,21 1 Ch.22-24 1 Ch.25,26 1 Ch.27-29	**Matthew** **21,22**	**Acts** **22-24**
Week 12 **19 - 25 Mar** 19 Mar 20 Mar 21 Mar 22 Mar 23 Mar 24 Mar 25 Mar	**Genesis** **47:28-50:26**	**2 Chronicles** **1-17** 2 Ch.1-3 2 Ch.4,5 2 Ch.6,7 2 Ch.8-10 2 Ch.11,12 2 Ch.13,14 2 Ch.15-17	**Matthew** **23,24**	**Acts** **25,26**
Week 13 **26 Mar - 1 Apr** 26 Mar 27 Mar 28 Mar 29 Mar 30 Mar 31 Mar 1 Apr	**Exodus** **1:1-6:1**	**2 Chronicles** **18-33** 2 Ch.18,19 2 Ch.20,21 2 Ch.22-24 2 Ch.25,26 2 Ch.27,28 2 Ch.29-31 2 Ch.32,33	**Matthew** **25**	**Acts** **27,28**
Week 14 **2 - 8 Apr** 2 Apr 3 Apr 4 Apr 5 Apr 6 Apr 7 Apr 8 Apr	**Exodus** **6:2-9:35**	**2 Chronicles** **34-36, 1 Ezra** **&** **2 Ezra (Ezra)** **1-5** 2 Ch.34-36 1 Ezra 1,2 1 Ezra 3,4 1 Ezra 5-7 1 Ezra 8,9 2 Ezra 1,2 2 Ezra 3-5	**Matthew** **26**	**Romans** **1-3**

Week 15 9 - 15 Apr 9 Apr 10 Apr 11 Apr 12 Apr 13 Apr 14 Apr 15 Apr	Exodus 10:1-13:16	2 Ezra (Ezra) 6-10 & Nehemiah 2 Ezra 6,7 2 Ezra 8-10 Neh.1-3 Neh.4,5 Neh.6-8 Neh.9,10 Neh.11-13	Matthew 27,28	Romans 4-7
Week 16 16 - 22 Apr 16 Apr 17 Apr 18 Apr 19 Apr 20 Apr 21 Apr 22 Apr	Exodus 13:17-17:16	Tobit & Judith 1-2 Tb.1,2 Tb.3,4 Tb.5-7 Tb.8,9 Tb.10,11 Tb.12--14 Jdt.1,2	Mark 1,2	Romans 8-10
Week 17 23 - 29 Apr 23 Apr 24 Apr 25 Apr 26 Apr 27 Apr 28 Apr 29 Apr	Exodus 18:1-20:23	Judith 3-16 & Esther 1-3 Jdt.3,4 Jdt.5-7 Jdt.8,9 Jdt.10,11 Jdt.12-14 Jdt.15,16 Es.1-3	Mark 3,4	Romans 11-14
Week 18 30 Apr - 6 May 30 Apr 1 May 2 May 3 May 4 May 5 May 6 May	Exodus 21:1-24:18	Esther 4-10 & 1 Maccabees 1-9 Es.4,5 Es.6,7 Es.8-10 1 Mc.1,2 1 Mc.3,4 1 Mc.5-7 1 Mc.8,9	Mark 5,6	Romans 15,16

Week 19 **7 - 13 May** 7 May 8 May 9 May 10 May 11 May 12 May 13 May	**Exodus 25:1-27:19**	**1 Maccabees 10-16 &** **2 Maccabees 1-10** 1 Mc.10,11 1 Mc.12-14 1 Mc.15,16 2 Mc.1-3 2 Mc.4,5 2 Mc.6,7 2 Mc.8-10	**Mark 7,8**	**1 Corinth-ians 1-4**
Week 20 **14 - 20 May** 14 May 15 May 16 May 17 May 18 May 19 May 20 May	**Exodus 27:20-30:10**	**2 Maccabees 11-15,** **3 Maccabees** **& Psalms 1-8** 2 Mc.11,12 2 Mc.13-15 3 Mc.1,2 3 Mc.3,4 3 Mc.5-7 Ps.1-4 Ps.5-8	**Mark 9,10**	**1 Corinth-ians 5-8**
Week 21 **21 - 27 May** 21 May 22 May 23 May 24 May 25 May 26 May 27 May	**Exodus 30:11-34:35**	**Psalms 9-36** Ps.9-12 Ps.13-16 Ps.17-20 Ps.21-24 Ps.25-28 Ps.29-32 Ps.33-36	**Mark 11,12**	**1 Corinth-ians 9-11**
Week 22 **28 May - 3 Jun** 28 May 29 May 30 May 31 May 1 Jun 2 Jun 3 Jun	**Exodus 35:1-38:20**	**Psalms 37-64** Ps.37-40 Ps.41-44 Ps.45-48 Ps.49-52 Ps.53-56 Ps.57-60 Ps.61-64	**Mark 13,14**	**1 Corinth-ians 12-14**

Week 23 4 - 10 Jun 4 Jun 5 Jun 6 Jun 7 Jun 8 Jun 9 Jun 10 Jun	Exodus 38:21-40:38	Psalms 65-92 Ps.65-68 Ps.69-72 Ps.73-76 Ps.77-80 Ps.81-84 Ps.85-88 Ps.89-92	Mark 15,16	1 Corinth- ians 15,16
Week 24 **11 - 17 Jun** 11 Jun 12 Jun 13 Jun 14 Jun 15 Jun 16 Jun 17 Jun	**Leviticus** **1:1-5:26**	**Psalms 93-110** Ps.93-96 Ps.97-100 Ps.101-104 Ps.105-108 Ps.109-112 Ps.113-116 Ps.117-110	**Luke** **1**	**2 Corinth-** **ians 1-4**
Week 25 **18 - 24 Jun** 18 Jun 19 Jun 20 Jun 21 Jun 22 Jun 23 Jun 24 Jun	**Leviticus** **6:1-8:36**	**Psalms 111-** **138** Ps.111-114 Ps.115-118 Ps.119 Ps.122-126 Ps.127-130 Ps.131-134 Ps.135-138	**Luke** **2,3**	**2 Corinth-** **ians 5-9**
Week 26 **25 Jun - 1 Jul** 25 Jun 26 Jun 27 Jun 28 Jun 29 Jun 30 Jun 1 Jul	**Leviticus** **9:1-11:47**	**Psalms 139-** **150** **& Job 1-10** Ps.139-142 Ps.143-146 Ps.147-150 Job 1-3 Job 4,5 Job 6,7 Job 8-10	**Luke** **4,5**	**2 Corinth-** **ians 10-13**

Week 27 2 - 8 Jul	Leviticus 12:1-13:59	Job 11-26	Luke 6,7	Galatians 1-3
2 Jul		Job 11,12		
3 Jul		Job 13,14		
4 Jul		Job 15-17		
5 Jul		Job 18,19		
6 Jul		Job 20,21		
7 Jul		Job 22-24		
8 Jul		Job 25,26		
Week 28 9 - 15 Jul	**Leviticus 14:1-15:33**	**Job 27-42**	**Luke 8.9**	**Galatians 4-6**
9 Jul		Job 27,28		
10 Jul		Job 29-31		
11 Jul		Job 32,33		
12 Jul		Job 34,35		
13 Jul		Job 36-38		
14 Jul		Job 39,40		
15 Jul		Job 41,42		
Week 29 16 - 22 Jul	**Leviticus 16:1-18:30**	**Proverbs 1-18**	**Luke 10,11**	**Ephesians 1-6**
16 Jul		Pr.1-3		
17 Jul		Pr.4,5		
18 Jul		Pr.6,7		
19 Jul		Pr.8-10		
20 Jul		Pr.11,12		
21 Jul		Pr.13,14		
22 Jul		Pr.15-18		
Week 30 23 - 29 Jul	**Leviticus 19:1-20:27**	**Proverbs 19-31 & Ecclesiastes 1-3**	**Luke 12,13**	**Philippians 1-4**
23 Jul		Pr.19,20		
24 Jul		Pr.21,22		
25 Jul		Pr.23-25		
26 Jul		Pr.26,27		
27 Jul		Pr.28,29		
28 Jul		Pr.30,31		
29 Jul		Ecc.1-3		

Week 31 30 Jul - 5 Aug 30 Jul 31 Jul 1 Aug 2 Aug 3 Aug 4 Aug 5 Aug	Leviticus 21:1-24:23	Ecclesiastes 4-12 & Song of Solomon Ecc.4,5 Ecc.6,7 Ecc.8-10 Ecc.11,12 SoS.1-3 SoS.4,5 SoS.6-8	Luke 14,15	Colossians 1-4
Week 32 6 - 12 Aug 6 Aug 7 Aug 8 Aug 9 Aug 10 Aug 11 Aug 12 Aug	Leviticus 25:1-26:2	Wisdom of Solomon 1-16 WSol.1,2 WSol.3,4 WSol.5-7 WSol.8,9 WSol.10,11 WSol.12-14 WSol.15,16	Luke 16,17	1 Thessalo- nians1-5
Week 33 13 - 19 Aug 13 Aug 14 Aug 15 Aug 16 Aug 17 Aug 18 Aug 19 Aug	Leviticus 26:3-27:34	Wisdom of Solomon 17- 19 & Wisdom of Sirach 1-14 WSol.17-19 WSir.1,2 WSir,3,4 WSir.5-7 WSir.8,9 WSir.10,11 WSir.12-14	Luke 18,19	2 Thessalo- nians1-3
Week 34 20 - 26 Aug 20 Aug 21 Aug 22 Aug 23 Aug 24 Aug 25 Aug 26 Aug	Numbers 1:1-4:20	Wisdom of Sirach 15-30 WSir.15,16 WSir.17,18 WSir.19-21 WSir.22,23 WSir.24,25 WSir.26-28 WSir.29,30	Luke 20,21	1 Timothy 1-4

Week 35 27 Aug - 2 Sep	**Numbers 4:21-7:89**	**Wisdom of Sirach 31-46**	**Luke 22,23**	**1 Timothy 5,6**
27 Aug		WSir.31,32		
28 Aug		WSir.33-35		
29 Aug		WSir.36,37		
30 Aug		WSir.38,39		
31 Aug		WSir.40-42		
1 Sep		WSir.43,44.		
2 Sep		WSir.45,46		
Week 36 3 - 9 Sep	**Numbers 8:1-12:16**	**Wisdom of Sirach 47-51 & Hosea 1-12**	**Luke 24**	**2 Timothy 1-4**
3 Sep		WSir.47-49		
4 Sep		WSir.50,51		
5 Sep		Hos.1,2		
6 Sep		Hos.3-5		
7 Sep		Hos.6,7		
8 Sep		Hos.8,9		
9 Sep		Hos.10-12		
Week 37 10 - 16 Sep	**Numbers 13:1-15:41**	**Hosea 13-14, Amos & Micah 1-4**	**John 1,2**	**Titus 1-3 & Philemon**
10 Sep		Hos.13,14		
11 Sep		Am.1,2		
12 Sep		Am.3-4		
13 Sep		Am.5,6		
14 Sep		Am.7-9		
15 Sep		Mi.1,2		
16 Sep		Mi.3,4		
Week 38 17 - 23 Sep	**Numbers 16:1-18:32**	**Micah 5-7, Joel, Obadiah, Jonah, Nahum & Habbakuk**	**John 3,4**	**Hebrews 1-4**
17 Sep		Mi.5-7		
18 Sep		Jo.1-3		
19 Sep		Ob.		
20 Sep		Jon.1,2		
21 Sep		Jon.3,4		
22 Sep		Nahum 1-3		
23 Sep		Hab.1-3		

Week 39 **24 - 30 Sep** 24 Sep 25 Sep 26 Sep 27 Sep 28 Sep 29 Sep 30 Sep	**Numbers** **19:1-22:1**	**Zephaniah, Haggai & Zechariah 1-12** Zeph.1-3 Hag.1,2 Zech.1,2 Zech.3-5 Zech.6,7 Zech.8,9 Zech.10-12	**John** **5,6**	**Hebrews** **5-8**
Week 40 **1 - 7 Oct** 1 Oct 2 Oct 3 Oct 4 Oct 5 Oct 6 Oct 7 Oct	**Numbers** **22:2-25:9**	**Zechariah 13-14, Malachi & Isaiah 1-10** Zech.13,14 Mal.1,2 Mal.3,4 Is.1-3 Is.4,5 Is.6,7 Is.8-10	**John** **7,8**	**Hebrews** **9,10**
Week 41 **8 - 14 Oct** 8 Oct 9 Oct 10 Oct 11 Oct 12 Oct 13 Oct 14 Oct	**Numbers** **25:10-30:1**	**Isaiah 11-26** Is.11,12 Is.13,14 Is.15-17 Is.18,19 Is.20,21 Is.22-24 Is.25,26	**John** **9,10**	**Hebrews** **11-13**
Week 42 **15 - 21 Oct** 15 Oct 16 Oct 17 Oct 18 Oct 19 Oct 20 Oct 21 Oct	**Numbers** **30:2-32:42**	**Isaiah 27-42** Is.27,28 Is.29-31 Is.32,33 Is.34,35 Is.36-38 Is.39,40 Is.41,42	**John** **11**	**James** **1-5**

Week 43 **22 - 28 Oct** 22 Oct 23 Oct 24 Oct 25 Oct 26 Oct 27 Oct 28 Oct	**Numbers** **33:1-36:13**	**Isaiah 43-59** Is.43,44 Is.45,46 Is.47,48 Is.49,50 Is.51,52 Is.53,54 Is.55,56	**John** **12**	**1 Peter** **1-5**
Week 44 **29 Oct - 4 Nov** 29 Oct 30 Oct 31 Oct 1 Nov 2 Nov 3 Nov 4 Nov	**Deuteronomy** **1:1-3:22**	**Isaiah 57-66** **& Jeremiah** **1-4** Is.57,58 Is.59,60 Is.61,62 Is.63,64 Is.65,66 Jer.1,2 Jer.3,4	**John** **13**	**2 Peter** **1-3**
Week 45 **5 - 11 Nov** 5 Nov 6 Nov 7 Nov 8 Nov 9 Nov 10 Nov 11 Nov	**Deuteronomy** **3:23-7:11**	**Jeremiah 5-18** Jer.5,6 Jer.7,8 Jer.9,10 Jer.11,12 Jer.13,14 Jer,15,16 Jer.17,18	**John** **14**	**1 John** **1-5**
Week 46 **12 - 18 Nov** 12 Nov 13 Nov 14 Nov 15 Nov 16 Nov 17 Nov 18 Nov	**Deuteronomy** **7:12-11:25**	**Jeremiah** **19-32** Jer.19,20 Jer.21,22 Jer.23,24 Jer.25,26 Jer.27,28 Jer.29,30 Jer.31,32	**John** **15**	**2 John,** **3 John** **& Jude**

Week 47 **19 - 25 Nov** 19 Nov 20 Nov 21 Nov 22 Nov 23 Nov 24 Nov 25 Nov	**Deuteronomy** **11:26-16:17**	**Jeremiah** **33-46** Jer.33,34 Jer.35,36 Jer.37,38 Jer.39,40 Jer.41,42 Jer.43,44 Jer.45,46	**John** **16**	**Revelation** **1-3**
Week 48 **26 Nov - 2 Dec** 26 Nov 27 Nov 28 Nov 29 Nov 30 Nov 1 Dec 2 Dec	**Deuteronomy** **16:18-21:9**	**Jeremiah 47-** **52, Baruch &** **Lamentations** Jer.47,48 Jer.49,50 Jer.51,52 Bar.1,2 Bar.3-5 Lam.1,2 Lam.3-5	**John** **17**	**Revelation** **4-7**
Week 49 **3 - 9 Dec** 3 Dec 4 Dec 5 Dec 6 Dec 7 Dec 8 Dec 9 Dec	**Deuteronomy** **21:10-25:19**	**Epistle of** **Jeremiah** **& Ezekiel 1-14** EJer. Ez.1-4 Ez.5,6 Ez.7,8 Ez.9,10 Ez.11,12 Ez.13,14	**John** **18**	**Revelation** **8-11**
Week 50 **10 - 16 Dec** 10 Dec 11 Dec 12 Dec 13 Dec 14 Dec 15 Dec 16 Dec	**Deuteronomy** **26:1-29:8**	**Ezekiel 15-28** Ez.15,16 Ez.17,18 Ez.19,20 Ez.21,22 Ez.23,24 Ez.25,26 Ez.27,28	**John** **19**	**Revelation** **12-15**

Week 51 17 - 23 Dec 17 Dec 18 Dec 19 Dec 20 Dec 21 Dec 22 Dec 23 Dec	Deuteronomy 29:9-30:20 Deuteronomy 31:1-31:30	Ezekiel 29-42 Ez.29,30 Ez.31,32 Ez.33,34 Ez.35,36 Ez.37,38 Ez.39,40 Ez.41,42	John 20	Revelation 16-18
Week 52 24-31 Dec 24 Dec 25 Dec 26 Dec 27 Dec 28 Dec 29 Dec 30 Dec 31 Dec	Deuteronomy 32:1-32:52; 33:1-34:12	Ezekiel 43-48 & Daniel Ez.43,44 Ez.45,46 Ez.47,48 Dan.1,2 Dan.3,4 Dan.5,6 Dan.7,8 Dan.9,12	John 21	Revelation 19-22

Note: 1 & 2 Ezra are also known as 1 & 2 Esdras

Abbreviations

Jos.	Joshua	
Jdg.	Judges	
Ru.	Ruth	
1Sa.	1 Samuel	(1 Kingdoms)
2Sa.	2 Samuel	(2 Kingdoms)
1Ki.	1 Kings	(3 Kingdoms)
2Ki.	2 Kings	(4 Kingdoms)
1Ch.	1 Chronicles	(1 Paraleipomenon)
2Ch.	2 Chronicles	(2 Paraleipomenon)
Neh.	Nehemiah	
Tb.	Tobit	
Jdt.	Judith	
Es.	Esther	

1Mc.	1 Maccabees
2Mc.	2 Maccabees
3Mc.	3 Maccabees
Ps.	Psalms
Pr.	Proverbs
Ecc.	Ecclesiastes
SoS.	Song of Songs
WSol.	Wisdom of Solomon
WSir.	Wisdom of Sirach
Hos.	Hosea
Am.	Amos
Mi.	Micah
Jo.	Joel
Ob.	Obadiah
Jon.	Jonah
Hab.	Habakkuk
Zeph.	Zephaniah
Hag.	Haggai
Zech.	Zechariah
Mal.	Malachi
Is.	Isaiah
Jer.	Jeremiah
Bar.	Baruch
Lam.	Lamentations of Jeremiah
EJer.	Epistle of Jeremiah
Ez.	Ezekiel
Dan.	Daniel

Use of the Calendar during festivals

Although no longer under the Law, the first Christian church observed all the festivals given by God and described in the Old Testament, these being fulfilled by Christ. For churches following this pattern today we advise that during the festivals, all of which have variable dates, the readings appointed are to be replaced by those of the festival. The calendar readings are followed again when the festival ends. Individuals may continue to read the designated passages in the calendar during festivals as part of their personal devotions.

APPENDIX B

THE BREAKING OF BREAD SERVICE

IN THE FIRST CHURCH OF JERUSALEM

An order for personal communion at any time

PREPARATION

Prepare your heart through remembrance of the Cross, repentance and forgiveness, to share in the body and blood of Christ.

Bread and wine are made ready.

BLESSING

One or more of the following blessings may be said:

> THE LORD LIVES! AND BLESSED BE MY ROCK, AND EXALTED BE THE GOD OF THE ROCK OF MY SALVATION!
>
> 2 Samuel 22:47

> BLESSED BE THE LORD GOD OF ISRAEL FROM EVERLASTING TO EVERLASTING!
>
> 1 Chronicles 16:36

BLESSED BE THE LORD GOD OF ISRAEL, WHO MADE HEAVEN AND EARTH.

2 Chronicles 2:12

BLESSED BE YOUR GLORIOUS NAME, WHICH IS EXALTED ABOVE ALL BLESSING AND PRAISE!

Nehemiah 9:5

BLESSED BE THE LORD, BECAUSE HE HAS HEARD THE VOICE OF MY SUPPLICATIONS!

Psalm 28:6

BLESSED BE THE LORD, WHO DAILY LOADS US WITH BENEFITS, THE GOD OF OUR SALVATION!

Psalm 68:19

BLESSED BE THE LORD GOD, THE GOD OF ISRAEL, WHO ONLY DOES WONDROUS THINGS! AND BLESSED BE HIS GLORIOUS NAME FOREVER! AND LET THE WHOLE EARTH BE FILLED WITH HIS GLORY. AMEN AND AMEN.

Psalm 72:18,19

BLESSED IS THE NAME OF THE LORD, NOW AND FOREVER.

Psalm 113:2

BLESSED IS THE GLORY OF THE LORD FROM HIS PLACE!

Ezekiel 3:12

BLESSED BE THE NAME OF GOD FOREVER AND EVER, FOR WISDOM AND MIGHT ARE HIS.

Daniel 2:20

An opening hymn or psalm of praise may be sung.

OUR FATHER

OUR FATHER,
WHO IS IN HEAVEN,
HALLOWED BE YOUR NAME,
YOUR KINGDOM COME,
YOUR WILL BE DONE,
ON EARTH, AS IT IS IN HEAVEN.
GIVE US THIS DAY OUR DAILY BREAD.
AND FORGIVE US OUR SINS,
AS WE FORGIVE THOSE WHO SIN AGAINST US.
AND LEAD US NOT INTO TEMPTATION,
BUT DELIVER US FROM THE EVIL ONE.
FOR YOURS IS THE KINGDOM,
THE POWER AND THE GLORY,
FOR EVER AND EVER.
AMEN.

From Matthew 6:9-13, Luke 11:2-4

PRAYER FOR ALL

A prayer for the salvation of all may be said, either extemporaneously, or using the following example:

REMEMBER IN YOUR MERCY, O GOD OUR SAVIOUR, ALL KINGS AND ALL THAT ARE IN AUTHORITY, THAT WE MAY LEAD A QUIET AND PEACEABLE LIFE IN ALL GODLINESS AND REVERENCE, FOR THIS IS GOOD AND ACCEPTABLE IN YOUR SIGHT.

BLESSED ARE YOU, LORD, WHO MAKES PEACE.

REMEMBER IN YOUR MERCY, O GOD OUR SAVIOUR, ALL THOSE WHOM YOU HAVE CREATED, WHETHER ALIVE IN THE BODY, OR DEPARTED THIS LIFE. WE PRAY FOR ALL, THAT YOU WILL VISIT AND HAVE MERCY UPON EACH ONE, YOU WHO DESIRE ALL TO BE SAVED AND TO COME TO THE KNOWLEDGE OF THE TRUTH. FOR THERE IS ONE GOD, AND ONE MEDIATOR BETWEEN GOD AND MEN, THE MAN CHRIST JESUS WHO GAVE HIMSELF A RANSOM FOR US ALL.

BLESSED ARE YOU, LORD, WHO MAKES THE DEAD ALIVE.

REMEMBER IN YOUR MERCY, O GOD OUR SAVIOUR, WE WHO CALL TO YOU NOW, THAT YOU WOULD VISIT US AND THOSE KNOWN TO US WHO ARE SUFFERING AT THIS TIME, THAT THROUGH THE MERITS OF YOUR CROSS WE MIGHT RECEIVE HEALING FROM SICKNESS, DELIVERANCE FROM AFFLICTION, AND GRACE TO HELP IN TIME OF NEED.

BLESSED ARE YOU, LORD, WHO HEARS PRAYER.

PRAYER OF CONSECRATION

A prayer of consecration may be said, either extemporaneously, or using the following example:

HEAVENLY FATHER, THANK YOU FOR BRINGING ME TO THE BEGINNING OF A NEW DAY. I GIVE MY DAY TO YOU, THAT YOUR WILL BE DONE IN ALL THINGS CONCERNING ME. I CONSECRATE MY ENTIRE LIFE TO YOU THIS DAY, TO GLORIFY YOU BY MY OBEDIENCE TO JESUS CHRIST, THROUGH THE POWER OF THE HOLY SPIRIT.

I GIVE MYSELF TO YOU AS A LIVING SACRIFICE, HOLDING NOTHING BACK. I WILL GO WHERE YOU SEND ME AND DO WHAT YOU COMMAND ME. GRANT ME GRACE TO FULFIL MY CALLING ON EARTH.

IN OBEDIENCE TO YOUR COMMAND THAT I RESIST THE DEVIL, I TAKE MY STAND TODAY IN YOUR STRONG TOWER AGAINST ALL SPIRITUAL FORCES OF EVIL THAT WOULD ATTACK ME, MY FAMILY, MY FRIENDS, ALL THOSE FOR WHOM I HAVE A DUTY OF CARE, MY WORK, MY CHURCH, MY NATION AND MY WORLD.

SUBMITTING MYSELF WHOLLY TO YOU FATHER, I OPPOSE YOU, FOUL FORCES, IN THE POWER OF JESUS' NAME, AND I BIND YOU ALL IN ALL YOUR OPERATIONS AGAINST US. TO GOD BE THE GLORY!

AMEN.

STATEMENT OF FAITH

CHRIST DIED FOR OUR SINS
IN ACCORDANCE WITH THE SCRIPTURES,
HE WAS BURIED,
AND HE WAS RAISED ON THE THIRD DAY
IN ACCORDANCE WITH THE SCRIPTURES.
HALLELUIA!

From 1 Corinthians 15:3,4

PSALMS, HYMNS AND SPIRITUAL SONGS

One or more psalms, hymns or choruses may be sung.

SINGING IN TONGUES

Praise and worship to God, singing in the Spirit.

A TIME OF HOLY SILENCE AND LISTENING TO GOD

Listening to God in stillness and silence, waiting upon Him until we have fully received what He would say to us this day, and taking note of what He says.

THE CRY OF THE SERAPHIM

HOLY, HOLY, HOLY IS THE LORD OF HOSTS;
THE WHOLE EARTH IS FULL OF HIS GLORY!

Isaiah 6:3

READING THE BIBLE

Bible reading, reflection and study. The calendar of daily scripture readings throughout the year may be used (Appendix A).

REPENTANCE

Silent reflection and repentance.

PRAYER FOR SPECIFIC NEEDS

Prayer for specific needs, including healing and deliverance.

THANKSGIVING

Giving thanks to God for the Cross.

A song or hymn on the Cross or on the blood of Jesus may be sung.

THE BREAKING OF BREAD

THE LORD JESUS ON THE SAME NIGHT IN WHICH HE WAS BETRAYED TOOK BREAD; AND WHEN HE HAD GIVEN THANKS, HE BROKE IT AND SAID, 'TAKE, EAT; THIS IS MY BODY WHICH IS BROKEN FOR YOU; DO THIS IN REMEMBRANCE OF ME.'

The bread is taken.

IN THE SAME MANNER HE ALSO TOOK THE CUP AFTER SUPPER, SAYING, 'THIS CUP IS THE NEW COVENANT IN MY BLOOD. THIS DO, AS OFTEN AS YOU DRINK IT, IN REMEMBRANCE OF ME.'

The wine is taken.

Having received the bread and wine, open your heart to God, asking Him to fill you afresh with His Holy Spirit.

THE BLESSING

THE LORD BLESS US, AND KEEP US. THE LORD MAKE HIS FACE SHINE UPON US, AND BE GRACIOUS TO US. THE LORD LIFT UP HIS COUNTENANCE UPON US, AND GIVE US PEACE. AMEN.

Numbers 6:24-26

A concluding hymn may be sung.

REFERENCES

REFERENCES

Alikin, V.A. The earliest history of the Christian gathering: Origin, development and content of the Christian gathering in the first to third centuries. Leiden: Brill, 2010.

Bradshaw, P.F. The search for the origins of Christian worship: sources and methods for the study of early liturgy. Oxford: Oxford University Press, 1992.

Bradshaw, P. & Johnson, M. The Eucharistic liturgies: Their evolution and interpretation. Collegeville, MN: Liturgical Press, 2012.

Cairns, E.E. Christianity through the centuries: A history of the Christian church. Grand Rapids, Michigan: Zondervan, 1981.

Chadwick, H. The early church. Harmondsworth: Penguin, 1967, 32.

Chadwick, H. The church in ancient society: From Galilee to Gregory the Great. Oxford: Oxford University Press, 2001.

Charlesworth, J. Jewish hymns, odes, and prayers (ca. 167 B.C.E. – 135 C.E.). In Kraft, R.A. & Nickelsburg, G.W.E. (Eds.), Early Judaism and its modern interpreters. Atlanta: Scholars Press, 1986.

Cullmann, O. Early Christian worship. London, 1953.

Dallimore, A. George Whitefield: The life and times of the great evangelist of the 18th century revival. Vol.2. Carlisle, Pennsylvania: The Banner of Truth Trust, 1980

Finkelstein, L. The Birkat Ha-Mazon, *The Jewish Quarterly Review*, 1929, 19(3), 211-262.

Hamman, A. (Ed.). Early Christian prayers. London: Longmans, 1961.

Happold, F.C. Mysticism: A study and an anthology. Harmondsworth: Penguin, 1970.

Lake, J.G. Communion service. In John G Lake: The complete collection of his life teachings, R. Liardon (Ed.), Tulsa, OK: Albury, 1999.

McGowan, A. Ancient Christian worship: Early church practices in social, historical, and theological perspective. Grand Rapids, MI: Baker Academic, 2014.

Messmer, A. Early Christian liturgy: A reconstruction of all known liturgical components and their respective order. *Journal of Biblical and Theological Studies*, 2019, 4(2).

Mickelson, J.K. Mickelson's enhanced Strong's Dictionaries of the Greek and Hebrew Testaments: English Dictionaries of the Textus Receptus, the 1550 Stephanus and 1525 Ben Chayyim. Living Son Press, 2015.

Palmer, W. Origines liturgicae. Oxford, 1832, 11.

Piédagnel, A. Cyrille de Jérusalem: chatéchèses mystagogiques. Paris: Sources Chretiennes, 1966, 161.

Ruth, L., Steenwyk, C., & Witvliet, J.D. Walking where Jesus walked. Grand Rapids, Michigan: Eerdmans, 2010.

Schurer, E. The history of the Jewish people in the age of Jesus Christ, Volume 2. G. Vermes, F. Millar and M. Black (Eds.). London: Bloomsbury, 2014.

Smith, D. From symposium to Eucharist: The banquet in the early Christian World. Minneapolis, MN: Fortress Press, 2003.

Spurgeon, C.H. Entry for 'Communion of the Saints'. In Charles Spurgeon's Illustration Collection. 1870.

Stormont, G. Wigglesworth: A man who walked with God. Tulsa, OK: Harrison House, 1989.

Tenney, M.C. New Testament Survey. Grand Rapids, Michigan: Eerdmans, 1961.

Turner, H.E.W. The historicity of the Gospels. Mowbrays, 1963.

Walker, P. Pilgrimage in the early church. In C. Bartholomew and F. Hughes (Eds.), Explorations in a Christian theology of pilgrimage. Burlington: Ashgate, 2004.

Wesley, J. Sermons on several occasions. London: Epworth Press, 1760.

NOTES

CPSIA information can be obtained
at www.ICGtesting.com
Printed in the USA
LVHW080104251120
672607LV00030B/922

9 780993 359927